WHAT EXPERTS ARE SAYING ABOUT *BABY SING & SIGN*®

"The combination of music and repetition is one of the best ways to teach language—or anything for that matter. And *Baby Sing & Sign* is a fabulous teaching aid. It's easy to follow; there are great practical tips; and Anne has a refreshing sense of humor and pleasant singing voice. Our 21-month-old loves to do the actions and practice saying the words. The first time your child uses one of the signs to ask for something, you'll know you've made a great choice."

—JIM "MR. STINKY FEET" COSGROVE
Children's entertainer and Warner Brothers recording artist

"It's wonderful to see encouragement to use 'real' signs to add to short, playful songs. Using just one or two signs per song keeps it successful and fun! Well done, Anne!"

—LYNN KLEINER
Founder and Director
Music Rhapsody

"*Baby Sing & Sign* builds on an infant or toddler's innate musical abilities and captures the essence of their eagerness to communicate. Dr. Miller encourages the reader to see life from the child's point of view, making it possible for a novice to access the information and immediately apply it in their interactions with small children."

—LYNN BRINCKMEYER, PhD
Texas State University
San Marcos, Texas

"I fell in love with the *Baby Sing & Sign* program instantly! My children and I love to dance about the house while singing and signing along with Anne's catchy tunes and beautiful voice! I love this program so much that I offer my community the opportunity to enjoy the *Baby Sing & Sign* program through Sign Language classes for little ones!"

—LIZ SAULT
ASL for Little Ones
Niagara Region Canada
www.aslforlittleones.com

"With twins, I find it is harder to keep them both occupied at the same time, as they always both want mommy's attention. Yet, they are very patient and will wait their turn if they know they are going to get a chance to hop on my lap and go for a ride in 'Miss Cassidy's or Mr. Cuyler's Buggy' (aka 'Miss Mary Jane'). My son especially loves 'The Walking Song' because he loves doing the sign for STOP. My children also love the song 'Roll the Ball,' and ask to listen to it on the CD, but much prefer to actually do it with someone. It touched my heart to come out to the kitchen one morning to find my older son, who also grew up doing baby sign language, leading his younger twin brother and sister in this activity. As a music therapy educator and parent of 'Baby Sing & Signers,' the benefits of this program are extensive, including language development, socialization, motor coordination, cognitive development, and of course musicianship!"

—CYNTHIA COLWELL DUNN, PhD
Director of Music Therapy
University of Kansas
Lawrence, Kansas

"Baby Sing & Sign is such a natural way for parents to encourage physical contact, interaction and language development with their children. I hope all parents take the opportunity to use this joyful and interactive tool that Anne Meeker Miller has lovingly developed."

—TERRY BUSCH, RNC, MS
Coordinator, Parent and Family Education
Shawnee Mission Medical Center
Shawnee Mission, Kansas

"Anne Miller has provided the perfect package for parents and teachers to enhance language development through simple, yet elegant music and baby signing activities....Music is the perfect vehicle for transporting language to infants and toddlers and *Baby Sing & Sign* provides a gentle ride for all."

—ELAINE BERNSDORF, PhD
Speech/Language Pathologist and Music Educator
Coauthor of The Music and Literacy Connection
Wichita, Kansas

WHAT PARENTS ARE SAYING ABOUT *BABY SING & SIGN*®

"Seeing your child sign for the first time is such an exciting experience. My little boy loved the interactive music and play activities so much! I also appreciated the inexpensive toy ideas. Our family loves *Baby Sing & Sign!*"
—SUSAN R.

"We often include the CD as part of our morning routine and can count on the songs to engage us each time we listen, sing and play along. The music provides a fun framework and inspiration for constructive play with our thirteen-month-old daughter, Ava. And, to quote my husband as he 'hops along like a bunny' with Ava, 'It's a hoot!'"
—KATE K.

"*Baby Sing & Sign* is one fun baby party! The music has encouraged my daughter's language development greatly."
—LINDSEY C.

"I am a firm believer in signing and singing with babies and did so with my daughter from the very beginning. I only wish I would have had your book instead of the one I used. *Baby Sing & Sign* is easy to read and enjoyable. I also loved your connection of literature to the signs—the teacher in me says: 'Way to go!'"
—AMY S.

"This multisensory approach to music and sign language encourages parents to give their children choices and allows them to explore their world. As an occupational therapist and a mother, I love the built-in repetition. I also love all of the practical ideas for making inexpensive instruments and toys!"
—SUSAN T.

"Great integration of signs and songs. Jake started clapping his hands to the music right away. He absolutely loves the songs on the music CD. He sits and stares at the stereo in anticipation when we put the music on!"

—JENNIFER W.

"My son loves the songs and CD. When we were driving back from the grandparents and he started to get a little fussy, I started singing the songs with him and he started smiling and just listening to me. Thanks for a great program!"

—CRYSTAL W.

"We play the CD almost every day, sometimes a couple of times a day, and my twins, Mason & McKenna, love it. They are starting to use their hands more and are getting close to signing some words like 'more' and 'ball.' Even if I don't have the CD or book near me, I sign the songs and use props to sing. They always start smiling and looking at me like they know the music and start moving, clapping, etc. Thank you so much for this wonderful tool to introduce language and interaction for my ten-month-old twins."

—KIM C.

"Taylor now signs during her tantrums to let us know what she wants. She also loves the CD when we're in the car. Her favorite signs are 'more' and 'eat.' It has really helped me feel comfortable when she is going to be away from me, I just tell our caretakers what sign means what and they're good to go. *Baby Sing & Sign* is a wonderful program!"

—HEATHER L.

"Our whole family has jumped on the *Baby Sing & Sign* bandwagon. Our six-year-old daughter is teaching grandma to sign. We love this program."

—KATHERINE G.

"How could there be a better baby gift?!"

—STEPHANIE F.

ANNE MEEKER MILLER, PhD

BABY SING & SIGN®

Communicate Early with Your Baby:

Learning Signs the Fun Way through Music and Play

Marlowe and Company
New York

BABY SING & SIGN®: *Communicate Early with Your Baby: Learning Signs the Fun Way through Music and Play*

Copyright © 2007 by Anne Meeker Miller.

Published by
Marlowe & Company
An Imprint of Avalon Publishing Group, Incorporated
245 West 17th Street • 11th Floor
New York, NY 10011-5300

AVALON

Library of Congress Cataloging-in-Publication Data is available

ISBN-10: 1-56924-254-2
ISBN-13: 978-1-56924-254-4

9 8 7 6 5 4 3 2 1

Designed by *Pauline Neuwirth, Neuwirth & Associates, Inc.*
Printed in the United States of America

I dedicate this book to my mother, Mary Anne (1935–2000), and my father, Don.
They made me the "folk-singin' mama" that I am today.

A portion of the proceeds from the sale of this book goes to non-profit organizations that support children's causes in the Kansas City area.

PARENTING PATIENCE
A Cautionary Tale

She was their first and only child,
Quite headstrong and a little wild,
And so it seemed to make no sense,
That for her name they'd picked Patience.

They'd carefully planned for their first child,
In hopes that she'd be sweet and mild,
They'd read each thing the experts wrote,
They'd gone to class and taken notes.

And so, they were quite sure they knew all the things that they should do,
Her mom ate right and walked each day, when she knew her child was on the way.
She gave up junk food and caffeine, the house was always nice and clean,
And she always tried her best to make sure she got lots of rest.

They hoped their child would be advanced, and they would not leave this to chance.
Starting three months before she was born, they read to her each night and morn.
They quit listening to country and rock, and replaced it with Mozart and Bach.
This would improve the baby's mind, she'd come out cultured and refined.

They knew that when the baby came, she might be influenced by her name.
It couldn't be just anything, and Patience had a certain ring.
Then one day the baby came, and life would never be the same.
For it is only fair to mention Patience wanted their attention.

From the day they brought her home, she hated to be left alone.
It was not difficult to tell for when they'd try, she'd start to yell.
She'd scream and shout and rant and rave (not how they'd hoped that she'd
    behave),
And it is only fair to say, she kept them running night and day.

When they'd hear their daughter call, the word that mattered most of all,
Was "when" (not who, what, why, or how) and by "when" I mean: "Right NOW!"
Her parents reread every book, and notes from classes that they took.
They'd followed the advice they'd read, and done each thing the experts said.

But though the experts were first rate, Patience would not cooperate.
They thought a child would be pure bliss; who knew it would turn out like this?
But of course you know it's true, not all were fooled, "their parents" knew,
For parents through the years have found, what comes around still goes around.

So future parents should beware, for children require special care,
And it is an awful shame, if you are fooled by someone's name.

CONTENTS

• • • • • • • •

FOREWORD

MUCH OF TODAY'S brain research has focused on infants and toddlers. The good news is that the continuing explosion of new information in this area has validated a lot of what mothers have always known to be true: the responsive, rhythmic dance of communication and connection between parent and child drives development. Ultimately it is *connection*—not the right toy or colorful mobile—that is at the core of human growth and development. We know that talking, singing, reading, and playing are essential for the healthy development of cognitive, social, language, and motor skills. We know that responding to our baby's cues and clues is the essence of good parenting. What we haven't known until more recently is the degree to which babies are capable of guiding and facilitating these processes.

Every parent, grandparent, and caregiver has played his or her fair share of trying to figure out what an infant or toddler wants or needs. We have our standard guesses: food, cuddles, diaper changing, and other needs. Eventually, we decode the child's gestures, gurgles, and grunts as we fine-tune our clue-reading skills. The temperament of the child determines how well he or she tolerates our learning curve. In *Baby Sing & Sign* Anne Meeker Miller uses the latest in brain-based learning and up-to-date knowledge of infant development to facilitate communication by empowering infants with sign language.

When I heard about teaching infants and toddlers sign language, my first thought was that we've exaggerated the benefits of brain research again. Closely following was my second thought: *This makes perfect sense!* Infants and toddlers understand more than they can communicate, and they already use gestures as a language system. Why not provide opportunities to deepen the language experience, empower the infant, and strengthen the adult-child bond?

I became an advocate when Anne first gave me her *Baby Sing & Sign* book and music CD. I passed it along to my neighbor, who had adopted a beautiful eighteen-month-old girl from China. After about a month, frustration had set in as the communication system between this loving family and their wonderful new addition was challenged by stress, mismatched cues, and cultural barriers. After two days with *Baby Sing & Sign,* harmony returned to the home as baby Melissa learned the signs for "more," "eat," and "stop."

What Anne has done with *Baby Sing & Sign* is nothing short of brilliant. She has joined  current research with the wisdom of the ages. The book you are holding combines music, teaching signs, and play to create fun activities that unite families; there could not be a more powerful combination to foster infant learning. Current research tells us that infants have surprising adultlike capabilities in the way they perceive and attend to musical stimuli. Human beings of any age are rhythmic, social beings with an innate need to communicate and connect with others. *Baby Sing & Sign* takes what nature dictates and creates activities that foster the developmental needs of children from six to twenty-four months of age. By pairing music with sign teaching, Anne provides a way to build in repetition and a meaningful context for learning a sign language vocabulary. This has special meaning for me, since at the wonderful age of fifty-four, I still find my way around the yellow pages by singing my A-B-C song from childhood.

As an author and speaker, I have come in contact with thousands of parents seeking to strengthen their bonds with their children. They intuitively know that strong connections foster cooperation and a plethora of developmental benefits. *Baby Sing & Sign* is an exceptional tool that empowers both infants and caregivers to communicate. Communication is the key to life. *Baby Sing & Sign* takes our precious babies on a journey from surviving to thriving. I wish you well on your journey with them.

—BECKY BAILEY, PhD
Author of *I Love You Rituals; Conscience Discipline*; and *Easy to Love, Difficult to Discipline*
www.consciousdiscipline.com
Oviedo, Florida, 2006

PREFACE

PARENTING CAN BE terrifying, heartwarming, irritating, rewarding, boring, and fascinating. Once we give birth to a child, we have to parent one way or another. We can make it glorious or devastating, but however we do it parenting is a learning experience. Our children learn from us. We learn from our children.

Why teach a baby to sign? Children actually attempt to sign and vocalize from the moment they are born, gesturing in their quest to build up a vocabulary, formulate sentences, and coordinate brain, heart, and tongue. A baby learns to communicate at an unbelievable speed, but there is a period when she cannot name her complex feelings and needs and the parent has not yet learned the meaning of all the sounds and gestures with which she tries to express herself.

Imagine yourself in a country where you don't speak the language. You need a drink of water, a doctor, a bed, or a lavatory. You speak the only language you know—and no one understands you. You become a child again as you attempt communication with your hands and body and wish there were an international language of some sort. Learning to sign tells your child, "I'm going to learn some of your way of talking and put myself in your shoes."

There are a number of sign languages, one of which is ASL (American Sign Language, used in this book). Signing is usually regarded solely as a means of communication for the hearing impaired. It lacks the subtlety of, but involves more of the body than, spoken language. Often the signer will mouth the words and move other parts of the body at the same time as signing so that varied methods of communication are employed. When I give a concert, signers often share the stage and they can be a delight to watch. They add a new dimension to any event, and the assembled company can learn the some of the signs as they listen—as happens in this book.

Baby Sing & Sign concentrates chiefly on nouns, verbs, and social niceties such as "please," "thank you," and so on. But unlike ASL, *Baby Sing & Sign* is intended for children who can hear—it adds sound to the mouth shape and the sign. The book focuses on signing at a basic everyday level, on the repetition and structure that create the familiarity and comfort needed by every child. Miller moves us on to combining the motions and speech with song. How lovely! So very different from (although complementary to) reading a book to your child, an activity in which the participants are looking at the same object rather than at one another.

A word about songs and about my mother, composer Ruth Crawford Seeger: she sang to us from our earliest days. We had songs for going to bed, for dressing, bathing, riding on buses, walking anywhere. She could make up songs or create new words for old songs at the drop of a hat. Many of the songs had hand, head, and arm play, a kind of ASL. Anything was grist for her mill: brussels sprouts, galoshes, afternoon naps, school. If you didn't want to do something, singing about it made it happen nonetheless. If you sang about it, it became something you wanted to do. Manipulation? Blackmail? No—just effortlessly effecting a change of direction. I did this with my own children, who can invent a song as easily as they eat or sleep.

On the CD that accompanies this book there is clear, no-nonsense singing. You and your child are encouraged to invent new words for the existing songs and to make new songs. You both become producers, not just consumers. One line of singing is a song. Two lines of singing are a longer song. Put your child's name in the song, his friend's shoes, her dog's tail. Keep in mind that children live in a world of detail, of particulars: the color of a dress, the shape of a toy, the names of things. The first-person singular is their most important person for now. You are of vital but secondary importance. What you are doing is helping your child's awareness to move out from self to the edges of the universe. You are creating his or her childhood.

Miller's mantra: parenting is not for wimps. It is the most important job we have as we enter an age where human behavior will probably determine whether the earth as we know it will survive. We need to raise our children into communicative, responsible, creative citizens. Not an easy job. Miller makes it more fun.

Just as important: babies are not wimps. Don't underestimate them. They are ever curious, so ready and able to learn that it is often hard to keep up with them. They absorb the world at every level, and they use all senses at once. Signing helps them develop speech. It may help you develop body skills you never thought you had.

Baby Sing & Sign is a children's book for parents, a kind of owner's manual. It keeps you on your toes and one step ahead of your little darlings. Use it. Enjoy it. It was written for you.

—Peggy Seeger
Singer and songmaker
www.pegseeger.com
Boston, July 2006

Ruth Crawford Seeger with her husband, Charles, and children, Mike and Peggy
(Photo reprinted with permission of the Seeger family.)

Ruth Crawford Seeger (1901–1953), mother of Peggy and Mike Seeger, was a premier pianist and music scholar and one of the first women composers of her day to be taken seriously. She collected and transcribed many of the familiar folksongs of our country and contributed to the folk music anthologies of Carl Sandburg and John and Alan Lomax. Her own *American Folk Songs for Children* remains a valuable resource for music teachers of young children.

Mrs. Seeger — or "Dio," as she was affectionately called by her family — created "Clap Your Hands" (Chapter One) with her preschool music students as part of their music play with the folk tune, "Old Joe Clark." She writes: "Many of the motions came first from the children; in the middle of a song someone would start tapping toes or stamping feet."

Said daughter, Peggy: "Our house echoed with love, clean clothes, good food, freedom, and evenings of singing." Ruth Seeger's legacy endures through her musical contributions and the treasured memories of her children and grandchildren.

To learn more, read *Ruth Crawford Seeger: A Composer's Search for American Music* by Judith Tick (Oxford University Press, 2000).

INTRODUCTION

KEVIN AND HIS mother are playing a guessing game. Kevin is a determined young man of thirteen months who wants something in the kitchen cabinet, and Mom is trying her best to figure out what that might be. She begins to list from memory all of the items in the cabinet that might be desirable to him: cookie, apple, milk, cracker? With each incorrect guess, Kevin's frustration level elevates. Pretty soon he adds foot stomping and loud squealing to his pointing game. His discontent is obvious, and his mother's frustration is growing. Various versions of this game are repeated dozens of times throughout the day.

Babies and toddlers are invested in their independence from the start. They are pleased that their known universe appears to be revolving around them, and they enjoy the numerous sources of entertainment and enlightenment the adults in their lives provide. They truly believe their babble is intelligible to your adult ear and try with all their baby might to communicate using their repertoire of facial expressions, body language, and vocalizations. Sometimes, of course, this is utterly charming! However, as illustrated in the example of Kevin and his mother, this process can often fall short of the communication needs for both parent and child.

Fortunately, there are ways to bridge this early communication gap. Long before their vocal mechanisms are mature enough to verbalize, babies can learn to communicate their wants and needs using gestures or signs. In fact, researchers have found that using sign language at an early age supports the natural development of the ability to speak. Babies who learn to sign experience less frustration and often verbalize sooner than their peers, and most important, sign language strengthens the bond between caregiver and child.

● ● ● ● ● ● ● ● ● ● ● ● ● ● ● ● ● ●

♪ WHAT SCIENCE SAYS ABOUT SINGING ♪ AND SIGNING WITH YOUR BABY

FOR THOSE INTERESTED in findings from the scientific community regarding sign language instruction and music in the lives of young children, here are a few excerpts from some notable research studies:

- Dr. Linda Acredolo and Dr. Susan Goodwyn launched the baby signs movement with their studies of language development in infants and toddlers. These studies have provided definitive research support for the effectiveness of using signs to communicate before a child is able to articulate words. According to Acredolo and Goodwyn, "Symbolic gestures are very similar, if not virtually equivalent, to early vocal words. They are used, just as early words are, to label objects as diverse as tractors and trees, rabbits and rain. And they are frequently combined with other symbols—including words—to communicate more complex ideas. In addition to these similarities in function we have also learned that both symbolic gestures and symbolic words arrive on the scene at the end of the first year, on average."

- Roberta Golinkoff and Kathy Hirsch-Pasek, coauthors of **How Babies Talk: The Magic and Mystery of Language in the First Three Years of Life**, explain why most children understand words but cannot speak them within the first year of life: "The infant vocal tract is not simply a miniature version of an adult's. Rather, it resembles the vocal tract of nonhuman primates. This prevents babies from using the mouth as an instrument in the ways necessary for speech. Not until the end of the first year of life, when the oral cavity has lengthened and expanded, are babies able to produce language sounds."

- In her book **Dancing With Words**, speech communication expert Marilyn Daniels found, "Students who receive sign instruction test significantly higher on the Peabody Picture Vocabulary Test than students in classes not receiving sign instruction. Their superior scores indicate that simultaneously presenting words visually, kinesthetically, and orally enhances a child's language development."

- Dr. Jayne Standley, whose pioneering work in the field of music therapy has led to new techniques for treating premature babies, notes: "The research literature on music enrichment for infants and toddlers has been prolific. We know that music participation teaches music skills, perception, and cognition. Simultaneously it also promotes child development areas such as listening skills, language development, motor coordination, cooperative social skills and reciprocity, demonstrating the power of music to be a highly beneficial reinforcer for children from the moment of their birth."

- Standley and fellow investigator Darcy DeLoach Walworth are currently incorporating the *Baby Sing & Sign* program in their research investigating how music can help infants born prematurely in acquiring language, social, and motor development skills. According to Walworth, "*Baby Sing & Sign* provides parents with the necessary tools to incorporate communication learning into the natural home environment where learning occurs the most successfully. The infants and parents attending our group sessions have responded positively to the combination of singing and learning new signs and have returned each week ready to learn new signs."

THE BABY SING & SIGN PROGRAM

Baby Sing & Sign is a unique approach to baby sign language and is ideal for busy families. The program uses music, pictures, and games to help you and your baby learn and practice a variety of simple and essential words from American Sign Language that can be used in meaningful communication with your child. The method is an outgrowth of my work as a music therapist for a public school system in the Kansas City area. Several years ago a colleague asked me about exploring the use of music as a way to help infants and toddlers learn to sign, so I wrote some child-friendly songs with lyrics that focused on key words, such as "Mommy," "Daddy," "please," and "want," which could be signed throughout the song. I soon found that music proved to be an incredibly engaging and motivating tool for learning sign language. Not only were babies responsive, but both they and their parents were also having fun!

The thirteen-song *Baby Sing & Sign* program described in this book is the result of my teaching experiences with infants and toddlers. Hundreds of young children and their caregivers—parents, grandparents, nannies, and others—have enjoyed the songs, signs, and play in a group setting by participating in *Baby Sing & Sign* classes. Now, with this book and CD, you can enjoy singing and signing with your baby at home.

♪ About the Signs

The signs and words included in the book were specifically selected to help children express their wants and needs. Using signs such as MORE and HELP gives babies the power to let caring adults know specifically what they desire. As children learn new signs, they begin to combine them to better communicate their intentions—MORE FOOD, HELP TOY. Animal and food signs are included because they are very motivating for young children to learn and use. Children love to point out animals they recognize in picture books, or at the park or zoo, and sign their names. And we all love our FOOD snacks—me included!

♪ About the Songs

The thirteen songs written or adapted for this book have a distinctively folksy feel. Each one provides opportunities to sing as well as sign the vocabulary included in the book. Some songs were composed for the program; others are slightly modified versions of traditional folk tunes. The melodies are simple but musically interesting to your baby—a child can recognize and respond to the tune and rhythm, and will delight in any new verses parents and caregivers may add to extend the fun and learning. For example, the "Doggie, Doggie" song could include verses about MOMMY and FOOD or BUNNY and BED.

When it is used as a language development program, I recommend singing these songs with infants from birth to two years. However, the tunes comprise a repertoire that can become a part of the entire family's tradition. The songs are inviting to children of all ages. Most of my *Baby Sing & Sign* parents have shared with me that the benefit of including the music in their family life has endured long after their children have learned to speak.

With each song presented in the book, you and your child will learn new signs and practice musical as well as communication skills that are playful and developmentally appropriate. And don't worry—no special equipment or training is needed. *Baby Sing & Sign* games use materials that are readily at hand and are easily assimilated into your daily routine. All that is necessary is a willingness to play and an interest in allowing your baby to direct his or her learning adventure!

HOW TO USE THIS BOOK

This book is much like Thanksgiving dinner: it is not intended to be consumed all in one sitting. The best plan for using, enjoying, and benefiting from *Baby Sing & Sign* with your child is to learn the songs and signs one at a time. Sing a tune with or without the CD until you know the lyrics well. Once both you and your child are familiar with the song, find the signs in the corresponding song chapter and introduce them to your child. The suggested games and books can be added to enhance the fun—in moderation and with good humor as you proceed.

Baby Sing & Sign is a process that allows you to capture your child's attention with music and teach sign language in such a playful way that children never realize they are learning a new skill. The program is designed to fit into your daily life with children and is meant to enhance—rather than complicate—your daily routine.

Following this introduction, which gives a brief overview of the *Baby Sing & Sign* program, you will find answers to frequently asked questions about sign language, music, and young children. "How to Sign with Your Baby" gives you the basics for teaching children how to sing and sign and illustrates the hand formations that will be used throughout the book.

Song chapters 1 through 13—the centerpiece of the book—appear in the order of the playlist on the *Baby Sing & Sign* music CD (found inside the back cover). Each song chapter consists of the following elements:

Song lyrics and specific suggestions for incorporating sign, movement and play while you sing, as well as a musical score with guitar chords.

"Tips for Introducing the Song" gives ideas for how to teach the song as well as how to teach the signs listed at the beginning of the chapter as "Words to Learn."

"More Musical Fun" describes additional activities designed to extend music and sign language learning while helping to maintain the child's interest.

"Games to Play" shows you how to make toys and play games with materials readily at hand in order to practice the sign language vocabulary. The activities can be customized to suit the developmental stage of your child and to help children grow in other areas, such as fine-motor and problem-solving skills. As a supplement to the infinite number and types of commercial toys, homemade toys are creative and inexpensive. Utilizing homemade toys for play also teaches your child that toys do not have to come from a store.

"Books to Read" lists a series of books recommended for infants and toddlers that fit the musical theme and vocabulary of a given chapter. Let this list be a starting point as you explore other titles at your local library or bookstore. Early reading experiences are wonderful for babies and toddlers and set the stage for their future literacy. Book engagement is an important predictor of reading success, as well as another effective way to practice sign language vocabulary. Take care not to overwhelm your child with sign language to avoid spoiling the closeness and security the child feels with you as you snuggle and read. Add signs gradually as you read books to your child. Repetition is necessary for learning the books as well as for understanding and using sign language.

"A Sign of Success" stories share thoughts about child development and parenting, and relate the experiences of parents and other caregivers who have participated in *Baby Sing & Sign* on their own or in classes. These vignettes are arranged in order of complexity—from the importance of being a patient teacher to the wonders of children expressing themselves through music and sign language.

For your convenience, I have included a *Baby Sing & Sign* dictionary containing all of the signs used in the book, along with photographs and instructions for performing them. This page can be duplicated so that you can keep a copy in your diaper bag or posted on your refrigerator door for quick reference. I have also included a glossary at the back of the book. Although everyday language has been used wherever possible, some terms that are commonly used in the discussion of language and child development have been included to ensure clarity and precision. These more "technical" terms are defined in the glossary. Finally, in the "References and Resources" section you will find lists of books and Web sites about language development and music for young children.

Here are some organizational features that are used throughout the book:

The pronouns "he" and "she" are used alternately to refer to babies and toddlers who will use the program.

Italics are used for safety reminders.

The book refers to parents and caregivers when describing caring adults who will use the program with children. Given the growing diversity of families, feel free to modify the song texts and other activities as needed to fit your family structure.

● ● ● ● ● ● ● ● ● ● ● ● ● ● ● ● ●

♪ A NOTE ON HOMEMADE TOYS ♪

Each of the song chapters in *Baby Sing & Sign* suggests games to play that reinforce the sign, and I sometimes suggest creating a homemade toy. When making and using homemade toys, the safety and well-being of your child are the first concerns. Please read the following points carefully before proceeding with any of the homemade toys described:

Homemade toys have not been subject to mandatory toy safety regulations. Please use your best judgment when preparing and playing with these items.

Infants and toddlers must be supervised at all times when using toys.

Babies put things in their mouths. Be sure toys are too large for them to choke on, are nontoxic, and have smooth surfaces.

As with all toys, check toys often to be certain they are safe for play.

● ● ● ● ● ● ● ● ● ● ● ● ● ● ● ● ●

· · · · · · · ·

THE BENEFITS OF *BABY SING & SIGN*
FREQUENTLY ASKED QUESTIONS

TO HELP YOU get a better feel for the nature and benefits of *Baby Sing & Sign,* I have solicited the opinions of some wise and experienced caregivers who have used the program, in addition to offering my own comments and observations. Here are some of the most commonly asked questions and answers.

Q: **What is *Baby Sing & Sign?***

Baby Sing & Sign is an enrichment program for infants and toddlers that is equal parts music, baby sign language, and play-based activities. The *Baby Sing & Sign* program supports the natural development of a child's language skills as she begins to make meaning of information, ideas, and social interactions that she experiences in her world. The music activities promote the child's emerging abilities to respond to the melodic, rhythmic, and expressive elements of music. Music is also used as a fun way to practice sign language vocabulary with your baby. The ultimate benefit is an enhanced bond between you and your child.

> "*Baby Sing & Sign* is the perfect mix of dynamic, fun songs and accompanying signs to teach parents and children how to communicate with each other. Learning to sign from your book and CD has made being Tabitha's mother even more fun. My initial cynicism about baby sign language vanished when I discovered your program and how helpful teaching my daughter to communicate can be."
>
> —GENEVIEVE B.

Q: **Will my child still learn to speak if I teach him to sign?**

Yes! Sign language provides an alternative to speech for children at a point in their physical development when their vocal mechanism is not mature enough to speak intelligibly. The ability to communicate through gesture gives the child experience in mastering the reciprocity, or "taking turns," aspect of language, as well as the gratification of expressing needs that are then met by caregivers. In my experience, children whom I have taught to sign stop signing words once they can say them clearly enough to be understood.

"We signed with Josie and Max. My biggest concern was that our kids wouldn't talk because they relied so heavily on signs. But that was not the case. Our parent educator was amazed at Josie's vocabulary and people still are. Max was even more advanced than Josie. At eighteen months, Max could say anything."

—STEPHANIE F.

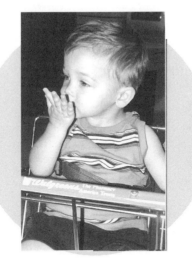

Kreg signs THANK YOU.

Q: **I thought sign language was only used to communicate with people who are deaf. Why should I use sign language with my hearing child?**

Babies have the ability to understand and communicate long before they are physically able to speak. Using signed gestures enables babies to "tell" caregivers what they want and need and therefore eliminates a lot of guesswork and frustration. Using the *Baby Sing & Sign* program creates a language- and music-rich learning environment.

"I look at my friends who have toddlers and I believe they are doing their child a disservice by NOT teaching them to sign. As a parent, my job is to help my child adapt and succeed in this world. By providing him with the means to communicate, I am validating my son's needs and desires. At eighteen months, Matthew is confident and patient and knows how to use the communication tools he has been given to his benefit."

—CASEY J.

Q: Who can use the *Baby Sing & Sign* program?

Parents, grandparents, teachers, babysitters, and day-care providers can all use the program with young children. The song material is appropriate for children from birth through the primary-grade levels. Although it is geared toward preverbal infants and toddlers, the program is ideal for any child or parent with an interest in learning to sign.

Experience in sign and song is an added benefit for children in home day-care or child-care facilities. Parents can be encouraged to play with their children at home to help them thoroughly master the skills.

"I run a home daycare business. I use *Baby Sing & Sign* with my children each day. It is part of our routine. I care for children of all ages, and they all enjoy the songs, signs and activities. I see offering the program to my families as another attractive feature for parents to consider when they are choosing childcare."

—ROBIN R.

Q: What is the best age for my child to start the *Baby Sing & Sign* program?

I recommend that you sing and play music to children from the first weeks of their lives—and even during pregnancy. Babies can actually hear a muted version of the world from inside the womb by the third trimester. My newborn son became noticeably calmer when I played recordings of my school choir at his bedtime. I believe he remembered the songs from listening to the choir rehearse during my pregnancy.

The beauty of the *Baby Sing & Sign* program is that it grows with the child and makes music a natural part of your lives together. During the first months of your child's life, take your time just singing and enjoying the songs. When baby is old enough to sit up, or around six months, you can begin introducing signs gradually as a part of your music making.

The child will begin to make sense of your gestures and start accumulating this knowledge in her baby brain. When she's around age ten to twelve months, you should then look for her to begin using the gestures in conversation with you. However, please remember that time frames are approximate, as each child is unique and may not conform to a predictable pattern for development in this or any other area. The *Baby Sing & Sign* program can also be beneficial to young children who are verbalizing. Gesture is a natural extension of both verbal and musical expression for children.

"We still nurse at bedtime and Riley enjoys playing with my hair to soothe herself to sleep. The other night we settled down to nurse and she reached for the nape of my neck to grasp a few strands of my hair. Then she did something she had never done before. She stopped nursing to sign 'thank you.' It was absolutely the most priceless moment. It was then that I understood how much Riley truly knows the connection between what she signs and wants to say. I didn't realize how much until that moment. Now she doesn't just communicate her wants and needs to me, but uses signs to express her appreciation also. I never could have guessed my toddler would be able to truly comprehend 'manners' or 'gratitude' at such a young age. Her signs have absolutely erupted the last month and she signs almost everything!"

—MARYLEE L.

Hannah signs BOOK.

Q: Did you make up the signs you teach?

The *Baby Sing & Sign* program uses American Sign Language (ASL) signs, but some of the gestures have been modified so that they are better suited to the fine-motor abilities of babies. I purposefully use this widely accepted system of signed communication, as when they are older it will enable many children to use their signing skills with peers who are hearing impaired or deaf.

Babies will not produce all the signs exactly as suggested in the book. Always accept their best approximation or attempt to sign, and treat it as the intended word. There are pictures of a young child signing modified versions of the ASL signs throughout the book. These are just examples of ways your child may perform the signs you teach.

> "I like the way that the **Baby Sing & Sign** program shows the way signs might be performed by my child, since it sometimes differs from the actual ASL signs. I probably would have missed signs done by my son if I hadn't been made aware of this. "
>
> —REBECCA G.

Q: Why do you use music to teach baby sign language?

Music is a great tool for teaching sign vocabulary, because it is inherently interesting and engaging to children. Active participation in music from an early age helps children realize their musical potential. In addition, both music and language give babies experience in detecting and organizing the patterns of sound, helping them to be focused and attentive listeners from an early age.

> "I began singing to Lana before she was born. My father was always singing and playing music as I grew up, so it just seemed natural. She seemed to respond to any music. I was a dance teacher at the time I was pregnant. Whenever music would play, I would feel my daughter move. After she was born, music was a daily and nightly ritual. She still falls asleep to music at night and her brother does the same thing. We sing in the car, on walks—any time! Singing and signing is an easy and natural way to teach your children language skills. It is also fun!"
>
> —NORMA F.

Q: How do I get started?

I suggest that you sing the songs to children first. When you feel they are familiar with the songs, you can teach the signs. To do so, take your cues from your child. Where does baby respond best to your music play? Sitting on your lap and bouncing, watching you at bath or mealtime, in the rocking chair at night, or while being held and dancing to one of your favorite tunes? Experiment with the best ways to maintain the child's eye contact and interest. This will set the stage and guide you as you begin to introduce signs. For more information on how to introduce the program and learn and teach the signs, see "How to Sign with Your Baby" (page 22).

> "My child is walking now and I can never seem to keep up with her! I find the best times for us to do our sign and music play are when she is in the highchair and at bedtime when we are snuggling in to read a book. I make our music and sign play sessions short and let her direct what song we sing and how we sing it—slow and smooth, or fast and bouncy!"
>
> —ROBERTA R.

Q: Is it difficult to learn the signs?

Teaching your baby to sign requires patience and consistency. As with all new skills, your child needs ample opportunity for practice and repetition of the signs in order to perform them and understand the connection to their experience. For example, many babies will learn to imitate the MORE sign by watching their parent and figuring out through trial and error how to get their two hands to come together in the middle to approximate this gesture. The more difficult step for the child is figuring out why his caring adults become gleeful when he puts his fingers together. Eventually he learns that by simply touching his fingertips, they will give him MORE of something he really wants. Once baby learns there is a desirable outcome to the business of moving fingers and hands, he will be very motivated to learn new signs.

Children typically understand language before they can express themselves by signing. If you were to explain electricity to me, I might be able to tell you that I understand your explanation. However, I would need to hear your explanation several times before I would attempt to explain electricity to someone else. The process of communication takes time and requires that parents and caregivers continue to say and sign the words—typically for months—before the child ever signs in return.

Baby Sing & Sign helps parents provide for repetition and practice by singing songs that include the sign language vocabulary they are teaching. Singing and signing is an easy fit. It is playful and fun, and both parent and child enjoy the activity together. It is easier for parents to be patient when families are singing and signing together. Waiting for the child's highly anticipated first sign becomes secondary to watching her enjoy the songs and participate enthusiastically by dancing, clapping, and vocalizing.

"As a mother and an occupational therapist, I love the creativity and thoroughness of this sensory-rich program. With another baby on the way, I am excited to give my daughter Ellie the advantage of learning to communicate her wants and needs at a young age. I loved having new songs to sing throughout our day in order to practice the sign language vocabulary as it naturally occurs in our routine: songs and signs for eating, playing, traveling, cuddling and reading. I was impressed with the movement and play integrated with the rhythm of the music, which helped Ellie develop motor and problem solving skills as she mastered her sign language words."

—TONYA G.

Q: I have twin infants and can hardly manage the parenting demands of their daily care. Can *Baby Sing & Sign* benefit parents like us who are overworked and overwhelmed?

Parenting is not for wimps! The demands and responsibilities that go with the job, compounded by frequent sleep deprivation, tax even the hardiest of us. But we do have one thing going for us: babies are fairly predictable. They crave structure and routine. They strive for independence while simultaneously refusing to let go of your pant leg. And they like the fruity baby food better than any of the pureed green vegetables.

Rather than adding new responsibilities, the *Baby Sing & Sign* program can actually help make parenting and caregiving easier, as your preverbal baby will soon be able to communicate his needs and desires with you through gestures. Babies who are able to communicate their desire for a drink, a snack, or a hug are less frustrated. Caregivers who are able to understand their child's needs and desires are also less frustrated. Ninety percent of parents surveyed named frustration at not knowing what their child wanted as a primary source of stress in their lives. (The other ten percent were too sleep-deprived to be able to hold a pencil and write legibly on the survey form!)

Baby Sing & Sign is easy to incorporate into your daily life. Chances are, singing and playing are already embedded in your child's everyday rituals: mealtime, car rides, bath and bedtime. And since the music and sign language activities engage and interest children, your baby will come to associate listening to your singing voice or the music CD with all things good and playful. *Baby Sing & Sign* is just the "spoonful of sugar" Mary Poppins was singing about when it was time for her charges to clean the playroom. Music becomes instrumental (no pun intended) in getting children willingly involved in the tasks of your life together.

The program can also help babies and toddlers transition from one activity to another. For example, you can sing and sign your way from playing with toys in the warmth and security of the family room to riding in the car to the grocery store. By redirecting baby from the reality of the dreaded shopping trip to the enjoyment of playing and singing with you in the car, you are able to minimize tantrums and discontent.

"I understand being overworked and overstressed, as I am the mother of thirteen-month-old twins. This can be very challenging! I try to use the signs as much as possible. It does not take any added effort. The twins are trying to verbalize what they want, and I help them by giving them the sign. Both of them have used signs for MORE and WANT. They have the biggest smiles when I repeat back to them what they signed. The rewards are amazing."

—MELISSA B.

"I have an active toddler and am in the final trimester of my pregnancy. Eric wears me out! I was dreading our drive to see my family for Thanksgiving, as my son doesn't tolerate his car seat very well. I anticipated five hours of screaming! We brought along our *Baby Sing & Sign* music CD and our son was happy for the entire car trip. The familiar tunes and the memory of the music games he and I play seemed to provide the comfort and interest he needed. He is an attentive listener when we sing or play the music, and we just saw him sign STOP and ALL-DONE for the first time when were singing 'The Walking Song' last week."

—SARAH L.

Jaclynn signs BUNNY

Q: I also have older children. Can I involve them in *Baby Sing & Sign?*

Involving the entire family in *Baby Sing & Sign* is absolutely recommended. Babies need to see what the signs look like on all of the hands in the household. They also benefit from observing signed conversation between family members. Older siblings are important role models, and the youngest children will work hard to imitate the behaviors of big sisters or brothers.

The musical material for the program is fun and interesting for children of all ages. Traditionally, folk music has been passed down from one generation to the next through oral transmission. That is, grandparents and parents sang to their children, and those children sang the same songs to their children and grandchildren when they grew up. Each family made the folk tunes their own by adding words or altering the melody. This active participation in music stands in stark contrast to the typical music participation today. We have become a nation of musical consumers, passively experiencing music by limiting ourselves to just listening.

Giving children songs they can sing to their own babies when they become parents someday is a wonderful gift. Activities that you share are memories in the making. Try to make singing and signing a family affair.

"I taught my daughter to sign, and she really took off with it. My second child, Sam, was slower to catch on. My daughter appointed herself the 'sign tutor' for her little brother. It was neat to watch her patiently instructing her brother in the hand shapes and their meanings. Sam responded thanks to my daughter and now has a sign vocabulary of twenty words. I love watching my children communicate with one another in their special language. My wife and I have benefited from my daughter's efforts, as Sam signs with us all now."

—DENNIS A.

Q: My child has a disability that makes it difficult for his speech to be understood. Can he benefit from the *Baby Sing & Sign* program?

Children with special needs often lack the oral-motor or language-processing ability to speak. Many parents have found this program to be an engaging and simple way to introduce sign language and to better facilitate communication. Just as with typically developing children, those with special needs benefit from learning a skill that allows them to express themselves and connect with caring adults.

American Sign Language is the primary means of communication for children who are deaf or hearing impaired. Sign language is also utilized in a program called "total communication," where parents and caregivers speak and sign simultaneously to the child, with the expectation that the child will reciprocate with sign. Hopefully, the child will use his voice to vocalize and eventually verbalize as he continues to sign. Once he is able to articulate words, he may drop the signing and speak instead. Total communication is used with children who, for a variety of reasons, are unable to talk. Medical conditions or situations that may delay speech include tracheotomy, side effects caused by chemotherapy, and language delay caused by premature birth. Other impairments and developmental delays that may warrant total communication include Down syndrome, autism, cerebral palsy, fetal alcohol syndrome, and aphasia.

"Anna suffered a massive brain hemorrhage in utero (cause unknown) and as a result has hydrocephalus, cerebral palsy, cortical visual impairment, as well as feeding and speech problems. Although her ability to understand language has developed typically, her ability to speak has progressed very little over the last two years. I know your program probably focuses on typically developing kids. However, I think sign and music are even more important to kids with developmental delays, as they have both been so instrumental in Anna's development. Anna absolutely loves music and has since the day she was born. It is often the only thing that will calm her during stressful times.

We often use music as a reward when trying to teach Anna new skills. It is a positive motivator for her because she loves it so much. Although Anna has limited use of her hands and is almost blind, she has learned about seven signs thus far, which have been invaluable. If a child with multiple disabilities like Anna can learn signs, any typically developing child can learn signs!"

—DIANA B.

Children who are adopted internationally can experience delays in speech due to language differences and the lack of a nurturing and stimulating environment during their infancy. Children often respond quickly to sign and song. In addition, musical experiences are a wonderful way to introduce a country's culture and customs. Sign language bridges the language gap between parent and child, and jump-starts their bonding process.

"Our daughter was thirteen months when we adopted her [from China], so she already had a good start on learning Mandarin. When she came to live with us, she didn't talk at all for quite some time. She definitely understood the gestures we used with her and responded incredibly to music. I don't consider myself to be a very good singer, but she was always in better spirits when I would sing to her. We believe she now talks better than most three-year-olds."

—SHARON AND KEN T.

"We adopted Faith when she was ten months old. She understands what we say to her, but it has taken a year for her speech to develop. We have tried different things to help her language develop, but believe sign language has been the most effective. Our daycare taught her to use MORE and that has given her a way to let us know her desires besides just grunting! She loves music and begins to move and smile immediately when we sing with her. Sign language and music have been invaluable to us for helping Faith with language learning and making the transition to our family."

—PAM K.

Hannah signs APPLE.

Q: When I look at the assortment of music CDs at the store produced specifically for children, I am overwhelmed and confused. What type of music should I play for my child?

It is important to involve babies in music making that is suited to their developmental needs. The growth and development of the brain depends on the quality and quantity of interactions children have with their environment, and for newborns much of this input comes through their ears. Listening to the sounds of the world and learning to turn toward a sound source come as children are able to integrate what they see, hear, and feel.

Quiet listening to a variety of music styles can be a positive experience for infants. Take care to control the loudness of the music, and try to find music that is soothing and contains predictable patterns that the baby can begin to organize and analyze in inquisitive baby fashion. Baby music should ideally contain a mixture of simple yet interesting material so that with repetition the baby will recognize and remember the tune. This book suggests ways to modify tunes that become familiar to baby in order to keep her musical mind engaged and growing.

The *Baby Sing & Sign* program provides active experiences in music and language play. When choosing music for listening to or singing with children, consider the following:

- Do the songs engage the child's mind, motor skills, and imagination?
- Are the elements (rhythm, melody, lyrics) and instruments the child hears simple

yet interesting and memorable?

- Can my child and I sing the songs and enjoy ourselves without having to play the recording?
- Are the tunes open-ended enough to allow our family or daycare to experiment with the rhythm, tempo, and words and make them our own?

Songs written for young children with adult listening preferences in mind have little to do with the musical needs of their intended audience. There are also songs that profess to meet the musical needs of babies and toddlers, but would bore any self-respecting youngster to tears.

Dr. John Feierabend has written several wonderful music books for young children (see the resources in the back of the book). He believes a song should be "delicious after many repetitions." If music is the food of love, play on!

Anthony signs CHEESE.

"I am a musician by profession, and am embarrassed to say that I didn't sing very much with my baby. The baby songs I knew bored me. I couldn't get excited about singing 'Twinkle, Twinkle Little Star' with my daughter. I needed songs that were interesting to me in order to get excited about singing with my baby. The songs in this book were playful and fun for us both."

—BRUCE V.

"My daughter especially loved 'Mommy Go 'Round the Sun' from the *Baby Sing & Sign* music CD. I sang her a special version with verses for every one of her friends and family members. She loved that we had our own special song. Of course, once you create a new song, you will need to include everyone each time you sing it. This can be both good and bad—good when I am trying to get all of her parts washed thoroughly in the bathtub, but bad when I am in a public place and don't feel like serenading everyone in the room!"

—KIRSTEN H.

Q: How does it feel to sign with babies and toddlers?

Enabling children to express their desires to the people who create the happiness and contentment in their world is a profoundly moving experience. It is amazing to see such little people direct the outcome of their daily activities by shaping their small hands. For both child and caregiver, their special "love language" is a powerful means of strengthening their bond. Sign language gives the caregiver a greater appreciation of the child's naturally developing ability to master communication.

"I wasn't convinced that my son would catch on to signed communication. I started using signs in my conversation with him when he was six months old. He didn't actually start signing until after his first birthday. I asked him if he wanted more water, and he signed ALL-DONE. It was such a small gesture—just a flick of his wrists—but I was blown away by the power of it! It made him feel so grown up to be able to communicate with his siblings. It was truly a satisfying experience for all of us. I wish I had signed with my other children."

—BOB M.

HOW TO SIGN
WITH YOUR BABY

T O BEGIN THE program, I suggest that you use the music CD as much as possible and sing to your baby. The music is easy to master and can be incorporated in your daily life from your baby's first month of life. Please set aside any misguided belief you may hold that you are not a good enough singer to sing to your child. She believes you are the best singer in the world. She associates you with smiles, kisses, good smells, and beautiful music. There is no voice she prefers to yours. Make singing a part of the loving rituals you establish with your baby.

Once you have listened to the CD and learned the tunes, you can alternate singing with or without the CD. Singing without musical accompaniment is called *a cappella* singing. Your a cappella singing will become a source of comfort and pleasure for your child as you softly sing your way through doctor's appointments, grocery trips, and car rides to grandma's house.

As you continue to enjoy the music together, take the time to read this book and practice the signs on your own. Baby's first six months are also a good time for making a few of the toys that are included in the song chapters. When baby is able to sit up unassisted, it is time to start your sign language instruction in earnest. Once the child sits up independently, his hands are free to begin to imitate gestures. However, it is perfectly fine to sign earlier if you would like. For instruction on physically teaching the signs, see "Hand Formations" below (page 24).

The chapters of the book are organized so that signs are presented in a sequence, beginning with those that are most motivating and useful for baby. However, you are encouraged to teach the signs and songs in any order you desire. Many parents and caregivers begin by teaching the sign for MORE, because it is motivating for baby to get what she desires and seems to do a good job of helping her understand the connection between gesture and word. In addition, it often provides a jump start for acquiring other sign vocabulary. I suggest that you begin with MORE and give the child several weeks before you add a new sign. If the child begins to use signs expressively, you can add words in quick succession. Much like Helen Keller in *The Miracle Worker,* once baby grasps the connection between gesture and word, she will want to know the sign for everything that is important in her world.

SPEECH DEVELOPMENT

Continue to speak when you sign. The goal of teaching babies sign language is to support the development of their speech. You are giving them the opportunity to "flex their language muscles" before their vocal mechanism is mature enough to speak, so it is essential that you combine speech with gesture.

Parents often worry about what to expect regarding their child's development of speech. When should my child be talking? How many words should she be saying and how often? This is particularly true when their first- or second-born child provides a point of comparison for their baby's language skills. Perhaps big brother or sister talked sooner or more often than baby. Most experts agree that in general firstborn and girl babies are the earliest to talk, and there is a wide range of what is considered to be normal language development in children.

Parents should also pay attention not only to what the baby expresses through sign language and speech, but how well the child understands and responds to what others say to him ("Where is the dog? Point to the dog in the picture"). The American Academy of Pediatrics suggests that by twenty-four months, toddlers should be able to combine two to three spoken words into sentences. They should also be able to follow simple instructions and repeat words they hear in conversation.

The goal of this book is to create activities that you can enjoy with your child while connecting with him in a more meaningful way. While research does suggest that the use of signing can enhance the overall communication skills for children, this may not be the case for every child. The activities and information in this book are in no way intended to substitute for the expertise and assistance of a speech-language pathologist, and are not meant to replace speech or language therapy. If you have any concerns about the development of your child, particularly in the area of communication, please talk to your pediatrician and/or contact your local school district for screening information.

HAND FORMATIONS

When introducing the signs, there are two techniques I use. The first I call "signing *on* the child." With the baby sitting in my lap, I say the word and perform the sign with my hands in front of the child. I then say and sign the word again, but use the child's body by either touching her face or manipulating her hands to sign. For instance, the word MORE is signed by touching gathered fingertips together. I would gently take the child's hands in mine and touch her fingertips together. I would then praise her for "using her words" to tell me MORE. To perform the sign for MOTHER, the thumb of the open hand is placed on the chin. I would say MOTHER and place the thumb of my open hand on the child's chin. This technique engages the child immediately because she wants to see what your hands are doing—it is a game she cannot resist.

The second technique I call "signing *with* the child" and requires that your baby is able to watch you sign, so be sure you are in his field of vision. Get down on your stomach if the child is sitting on the floor, or sign to your child when he is in a high chair or grocery cart. Babies love faces, so make sure you use lots of facial expression as you say and sign words for the child to see. You can also prompt the child to perform the signs when talking face-to-face by taking his little hands and moving them as you say the word you sign. Then smile and thank him for "telling" you the word. He will also appreciate applause and enthusiasm for each new word he signs.

The adult model in pictures throughout the book demonstrates the vocabulary using American Sign Language (ASL). For the purpose of teaching you the basic baby sign vocabulary, here are some key hand formations that you can practice. When referred to in the book, hand formations appear in italics.

Flat hand or closed fingers

Gathered fingertips

Closed two fingers

Open two fingers

Closed fist

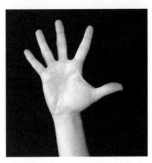

Open fingers

Note that teaching finger spelling and extensive ASL vocabulary is beyond the scope of this book. If you are interested in learning ASL in more depth, there are courses that may be available to you in your community that teach the grammar, syntax, and vocabulary unique to American Sign Language, which is utilized in communication with most deaf adults. In addition, Michigan State University has developed a Web site called American Sign Language Vocabulary Browser (see "References and Resources" in the back of the book) that provides short video clips of thousands of signs. Many parents find this Web site helpful in learning new signs to teach baby that have meaning and importance for their family.

GETTING STARTED

As you begin signing with your baby, keep these tips in mind:

○ Teach one sign at a time. Progress slowly so that your child can learn "deeply" the sign you are presenting and move from simply recognizing the sign to comprehending its meaning.

○ Always speak as well as sign the word. You are teaching your child to respond to both your verbal and signed communication.

○ You may use either hand to form the signs.

○ Use facial expressions that reinforce what you are trying to communicate.

○ Give your baby adequate time to respond before repeating signs.

○ Continue to sign to your child even if he does not sign to you. Although you may not see your child forming signs and using them to communicate with you, he most likely understands the words and signs you use to communicate with him.

○ Look for an approximation or "best try" as your child attempts to imitate the signs you teach.

○ Be positive and encouraging. Don't forget to have fun!

SIGNING WITH BOOKS

It is never too early to teach children a love for books. Just as music communicates deep feelings and ideas in a manner that words cannot, books have a unique power to engage the mind and the imagination. Perhaps one of the reasons that babies love books is because it gives them something to both see and hear—they can listen to their favorite voices read them the words as they look at the colorful and interesting pages. Over time, the pictures become recognizable to children as representations of important objects and experiences in their world. They love to pause to point to things they recognize when asked: "Where is the picture of the CAT on this page? Touch the picture of the APPLE on that page."

With lots of repetition, the child begins to anticipate the events in the story and develops the ability to predict what happens next. Her attention moves from identifying items pictured to wanting to turn the page to make sure that the page with the BOY playing MUSIC will be followed by the page with the DOG barking a tune. She will also start to look at the pictures on the page from left to right just as she will someday do when it is time to read words.

A child's ability to point to pictures that have meaning for her, to anticipate events in a story, and to follow the story from the left page to the right are all important skills for future reading success. Reading books also supports the goal of sign language learning, as this special time between you and your baby affords you a wonderful opportunity to sign as you read. This is typically a time when baby is quiet and focused on you and the book you are prepared to share. Place the child on your lap facing out, set the book in your lap, and use your hands in front of her body to sign key vocabulary words you find in the text.

To enhance the sign language learning during reading time, make sure you choose books that have rhyme and repetition. You can always repeat the signed words on the page for extra practice. Be creative in including sign vocabulary by changing a word or two in the text to include more of the signs you wish to teach. You will be able to get away with this for a few more years until she starts to memorize the text and scolds you for reading it "wrong."

One of the unique benefits of singing and signing with babies is that the music provides a meaningful and enjoyable context for repeating and practicing the sign vocabulary. Book reading accomplishes the same goal. With lots of repetition, your child will learn to turn the pages of her favorite book and sign the words you have practiced together.

Megan will demonstrate signs based on American Sign Language (ASL).

Lana will show some of the possible modifications a child might make to the ASL signs.

SECRETS OF SUCCESS WITH SINGING AND SIGNING

○ Let your child direct you in selecting signs that have importance for her. Your child may have an affinity for playing BALL or may adore your family's DOG. Start with what she cares about most.

○ Make your sign teaching a natural part of your day. Language learning requires a meaningful context.

○ Take "baby steps" in incorporating the ideas from this book into your child's life. Play with a sign and a song for as long as it takes for both of you to feel confident you have mastered the material.

○ You will undoubtedly tire of the songs and activities long before your child. But the goal is to support your child's typical language development process by teaching signed communication skills, and that involves practice. Remember: *Repetition is good. Repetition is good. Repetition is good.*

○ Remind yourself often that the real reason for doing baby sign language and music with your child is to have fun!

Isaac and mom are "having a ball" learning to sign BALL!

CLAP YOUR HANDS

WORDS TO LEARN: **MORE, MUSIC**

Clap, clap, clap your hands,	*Clap hands*
Clap your hands together,	*Clap hands*
Clap, clap, clap your hands,	*Clap hands*
Clap your hands together.	*Clap hands*
La la la . . .	*Sign MUSIC to the beat*
Verse 2. Stomp, stomp, stomp your feet	*Stomp feet or move child's feet rhythmically to the beat*
Verse 3. Move, move, move your head	*Move head or move child's head gently with your hands*
Verse 4. Dance, dance, dance with me	*Dance while holding child, or bounce child gently in lap, or hold child underneath his arms and lift him up and down so that he can bounce on the ground with his feet*
Verse 5. Run, run, run with me	*Run in place while holding child, bounce child on your lap, or lift him up and down so that he can bounce on the ground with his feet*

CLAP YOUR HANDS

American Folk Songs for Children by Ruth Crawford Seeger.
Copyright © 2002 by Mike Seeger
All rights reserved. Adapted by Anne Meeker Miller

MORE

Tap gathered fingertips of both hands together several times.

Naomi's version of MORE includes one open hand. Look for your baby's approximation of the sign you demonstrate.

MUSIC

Wave the palm of one flat hand over the other extended arm held with palm up. Sweep hand back and forth from wrist to shoulder.

To simplify the gesture, child may wave arm in the air without crossing her body to her extended arm.

TIPS FOR INTRODUCING *CLAP YOUR HANDS*

○ This joyful, upbeat folk tune requires little explanation. Allow the lyrics to lead you as you move to the music.

○ Sign MUSIC as each instrument plays a solo on the "la" passages of the song.

○ Babies will need some gentle assistance to perform the claps. You can make the song into a bounce on your lap, gently jostling her as you stomp your feet and "run with me." See if the child will imitate your head movements on "move your head."

○ Ask your child if she would like MORE "Clap Your Hands." Help her form the sign for MORE with her hands. Thank your child for signing MORE. Then sing the song again from the top!

♪ More Musical Fun with *Clap Your Hands*

● The "la" passages in between verses present an opportunity for your child to improvise some moves of his own. Observe him to see if he is beginning to anticipate this repeating section of the song. For example, babies may begin to kick their legs or move their arms. You can then sing a special "kick your feet" verse just for baby. Toddlers may alter their movements in expectation of the returning "la's."

● You can pantomime playing the different instruments you hear during the interlude.

● "Clap Your Hands" is a wonderful song to incorporate into the activities of your daily life. There are countless verses you and your child can create: roll the ball, take a bath, or brush your teeth (tooth if it is a small baby). Be sure to sing the "la" passage with enthusiasm!

● This song is also a good way to observe your child's ability to understand language. Is she clapping her hands when she hears the "clap your hand" song lyric? Does she follow the instructions the music playfully provides? The child needs to be able to understand your words—signed and spoken—before she will be able to begin to gesture meaningfully.

GAMES TO PLAY

♪ Bells on Her Fingers and Bells on His Toes

VOCABULARY PRACTICE: MUSIC, MORE
DEVELOPMENTAL BENEFITS: motor skills, awareness of sound
MATERIALS: elastic, needle and thread, jingle bells, stuffed toy animal

DIRECTIONS: Sew the ends of the elastic together to form ankle and wrist bracelets. Make sure the elastic is not too tight. Sew jingle bells securely onto the elastic bands. Place the bracelets around your child's ankles and wrists. Play the recording of "Clap Your Hands" and help your baby shake the bells. Provide lots of happy facial expression and giggles. Stop the music and ask your child if she would like MORE.

Hold your child tight and take her for a spin on your dance floor cleared of furniture and other potential obstacles. Tell your child how much you like MUSIC and dancing with her. Be sure to do some gentle dips and spins to maximize the jingles and jangles of the bells. Perhaps a stuffed animal might like to wear the jingle bells and do a fancy dance, too. Let your child "dance" the toy around! *NOTE: As with all the activities described in this book, it is important that adults supervise children carefully to keep them safe as they learn and explore. Jingle bells used for this activity could become a choking hazard for your child if they found their way to his mouth.*

Clapping is a natural way for babies to express pleasure, and is one of the first "signs" your child will perform.

♪ Musical Pictures

VOCABULARY PRACTICE: MUSIC

DEVELOPMENTAL BENEFITS: use of pictures to create meaning, focused listening and looking

MATERIALS: trading card plastic protector sheet, index cards, glue, instrument pictures

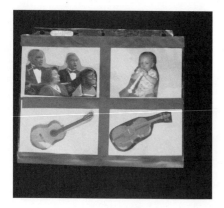

DIRECTIONS: Many toddlers enjoy an instrument picture game. Find pictures of the instruments on the Internet or in magazines, and paste them onto paper or index cards. Slip the cards into the pockets of a trading card plastic protector sheet. These are inexpensive and can be purchased from an office supply store or your local Wal-Mart. (Buy several, because there are other ways to use them described in this book.)

Some of the instruments you hear on the music CD include guitar, mandolin (small string instrument played like a guitar), flute, and violin, in addition to singing. Ask your child to point to MUSIC. Ask him to listen to the MUSIC.

♪ Laundry Basket Swing

VOCABULARY PRACTICE: MORE, MUSIC

DEVELOPMENTAL BENEFITS: awareness of cause and effect, social interaction, musical play

MATERIALS: laundry basket, blanket

DIRECTIONS: Use blankets to pad a laundry basket to fit the size of your child. Place the child in the basket. Hold the laundry basket with another adult partner and swing the child gently. Create a melody for a simple lyric such as "swing, swing, swing" to the rhythm of your swinging. Set the child down and ask if she would like MORE swinging. Help your child form the MORE sign. Tell your child, "Good job signing MORE," then continue the swinging game.

Children enjoy practicing their sign language vocabulary with the Laundry Basket Swing game.

A SIGN OF SUCCESS

♪ YOUR BABY UNDERSTANDS LANGUAGE BEFORE ♪ SHE CAN EXPRESS IT

Train up a child in the way he should go: and when he is old,
he will not depart from it.
—PROVERBS 22:6

A child's experience in early life is crucial for later cognitive, emotional, physical, and psychological development. The same holds true for experiencing language. From their earliest days, nothing is more important to babies than the sound of their parents' voices. It is through talking and interacting on a daily basis that their language abilities develop and grow.

It's never too early to begin imprinting your baby's brain, so don't feel embarrassed when other shoppers give you odd looks as you push your cart down the grocery store aisle, discussing with your newborn which brand of spaghetti sauce you prefer and why. That's because *receptive language*—the ability to understand words—develops before the ability to speak and use words. Child development specialists are discovering that even the youngest infants are capable of understanding what is being said to them, even if only through a parent's facial expressions or tone of voice. And by six to eight months of age, most babies understand what certain words mean.

> It is through talking and interacting on a daily basis that children's language abilities develop and grow.

Amy began signing to her daughter, Isabella, long before her child had the ability to sign back, because she found it was an excellent way to connect symbols to the particular words she was using with her infant daughter over and over throughout the day. Although Isabella did not sign back for many months, Amy knew her daughter was developing receptive language by the way she would respond to certain signs. For example, when her mother signed MILK or EAT before her morning meal, Isabella would babble with delight and move her hands and feet in a display of happiness. Also, Amy used the sign for HELP whenever she saw Isabella becoming frustrated. The infant would appear to calm down, as if knowing that her mother understood her frustration and would try to help with whatever was distressing her.

Kendall began signing to her son, Isaac, right after he was born. When their son was five months old, she and her husband made an extra effort to focus on practicing sign language by consistently combining several spoken words with signs in everyday routines, and they believe that Isaac began understanding the meaning of these word/sign combinations within a month or two.

In addition to her tour of duty as a devoted mom, Kendall has a college degree in early childhood development and works with young children in a local school district. She once worked with an autistic student who at age two had no expressive language. Seven years later Kendall reunited with the student, now age nine, and found the child's expressive language had greatly improved. She discovered that her former student could talk about things he remembered from when he was much younger; another example of how children—any child—can understand language even when they don't participate in it through verbal communication.

So don't feel silly the next time you have a heart-to-heart talk with your infant. She might relate.

Your child must learn to imitate your actions before he can begin to sign.

BOOKS TO READ

Babies love animals. And *The Animal's Song* by David Harrison (Boyds Mills Press) is doubly delightful because it combines a variety of kids and critters with MUSIC to create a creature chorus certain to delight young readers. The repetitious verses will help baby master the form and cadence of the verse. Sign MUSIC and use your singing voice for all the italicized animal sounds. DOG (chapter 4) and BOY and GIRL (chapter 7) are also included in the story, so be certain to read the book again when you have learned the signs.

MORE

How Many Kisses Do You Want Tonight? by Vasha Bajaj (Little, Brown)

The Hungry Caterpillar by Eric Carle (Philomel Books)

Bear Wants More by Karma Wilson and Jane Chapman (Scholastic)

I Love You More by Judy Cooley (Shadow Mountain)

I Love You More by Laura Duksta and Karen Keelser (I Shine)

"More, More, More," Said the Baby by Vera B. Williams (HarperFestival)

More Please: The Hungry Animal Book by Dorothy Kunhardt (Golden Books)

MUSIC

Animal Music by Harriet Ziefert (Houghton Mifflin)

Baby Danced the Polka by Karen Beaumont (Dial Books for Young Readers)

Clap Your Hands by Lorinda Cauley (Putnam Publications Group)

Clap Your Hands by David Ellwand (Handprint Books)

Pots and Pans by Patricia Hubbell (HarperCollins)

Snow Music by Lynne Rae Perkins (Greenwillow)

We All Sing with the Same Voice by J. Philip Miller and Sheppard M. Greene (HarperCollins)

THIS IS THE MOMMY WIGGLE

WORDS TO LEARN: **MOMMY, DADDY**
WORD TO REVIEW: **MUSIC**

This is the mommy sweet as can be.	*Sign MOMMY*
This is the daddy	*Sign DADDY*
who snuggles with me.	*Sign I LOVE YOU* (hug self)*
This is the sister—she loves to play.	*Sign PLAY**
This is the brother who shouts "Hooray!"	*Lift fist in the air*
This is the baby who thinks she's Queen [or he's King],	*Point to your baby girl or boy*
And this is the song that they love to sing:	*Sign MUSIC*
La la la la, la, la, la, la, la	*Sign MUSIC*

*Add **PLAY** and **I LOVE YOU** signs to the performance of this tune after they have been presented (chapter 3: PLAY; chapter 13: **I LOVE YOU**).

THIS IS THE MOMMY WIGGLE

Sung to the tune of
"Twinkle, Twinkle Little Star"
Adapted by Anne Meeker Miller

MOMMY

Place thumb of open fingers on chin.

Child may tap or point to her chin.

DADDY

Place thumb of open fingers on forehead.

Child may tap or point to her forehead.

TIPS FOR INTRODUCING
THIS IS THE MOMMY WIGGLE

○ You probably remember playing "This Little Piggie," where you touch and wiggle baby's toes or fingers. "Wiggles" are popular baby games, and hundreds of them are recorded in American folklore. Our version can be played as a traditional "wiggle" where one finger or toe is touched for each person in the song. You can touch baby's fingers as you share the text, or you can show the baby your fingers. Be sure to sign MOMMY, DADDY, and MUSIC after you touch his fingers or toes.

○ I wrote this updated variation of the old finger play. For example, there is no longer a "short, stout" mother or sister who only plays with dolls. The "baby king" lyric refers to our special name for my third son. Although we tried not to spoil him, he had both of his big brothers doing his bidding from the start.

○ After you finish singing this song, say "Do you want MORE?" as you sign MORE. Then prompt your child to sign MORE. Tell your child, "Good signing MORE," and repeat the song.

♪ More Musical Fun with *This Is the Mommy Wiggle*

● Babies prefer songs with a quick tempo, so sing lively!

● Try making this wiggle into a bounce. Turn baby around so that she is facing you. Take her hands in yours or hold her around her rib cage.

● Gently bounce your baby on your thighs as you sing or speak the rhyme. Older children might like to slide down your legs on the descending "la" refrain. Babies can gently recline with their head supported by your hand.

● Babies who enjoy being tickled will like it if your fingers walk down their arm from shoulder to wrist on the descending "la" passage. Tickle your baby's hand and tummy when you get to the last note.

GAMES TO PLAY

♪ The Royal Treatment

VOCABULARY PRACTICE: **MOMMY, DADDY, MORE, MUSIC**
DEVELOPMENTAL BENEFITS: imaginative play
MATERIALS: paper crown

DIRECTIONS: Give your baby the "royal treatment." Make a crown for your child or procure one from your local Burger King.

Place the crown on the head of your "queen" or "king" as you perform this wiggle. Ask your baby if she is MOMMY'S or DADDY'S queen. Be prepared to serve as her court jester and provide MORE MUSIC.

The "Baby King" requires his grandfather do his bidding well.

♪ Baby's Fun Feast

VOCABULARY PRACTICE: **MOMMY, DADDY, MUSIC**
DEVELOPMENTAL BENEFITS: use of pictures to create meaning
MATERIALS: trading card plastic protector sheet, pictures of family members

DIRECTIONS: Insert photographs of MOMMY, DADDY, sister, brother, and baby in the pockets of a trading card plastic protector sheet. Now you have a fun "baby placemat" to use when you are practicing this song.

Ten out of ten babies surveyed love to look at photographs of their families.

As you sing and sign the song, point to each family member's photograph. The picture mat is also a great diversion for your baby as you prepare her meal. Place it on her high chair tray and sing as you dish up dinner. Baby can "read" her MUSIC while you are singing and preparing her food.

♪ Zip-Lock Book

VOCABULARY PRACTICE: **MOMMY, DADDY**

DEVELOPMENTAL BENEFITS: book handling and engagement, use of pictures to create meaning

MATERIALS: Four or five resealable quart-size sandwich bags; construction paper; pictures from magazines or coloring books, or photographs; markers; glue; needle and thread; scissors; cloth tape (we used colored electrician's tape over staples)

DIRECTIONS: To create this special book:

1. Cut a piece of construction paper to fit inside each bag, about three-quarters of an inch shorter and narrower than the bag.
2. Glue a picture or photograph to each page or draw your own.
3. Slip each page into a bag, with the open end of the bag at the right. Zip the bag closed.
4. Sew the unopened ends of two bags together securely with needle and thread, or staple together. Now you have a spread consisting of two pages.
5. Cover the sewn or stapled side with cloth tape.
6. Continue with other pages. If you have a sewing machine, you can easily sew across the edge of four or five stacked bags at the same time.

Start with pictures of MOMMY and DADDY in the book. Ask your child to touch the person you name. Change the pictures periodically as your child's vocabulary grows, and ask him to touch or tell you the names of the people and things he sees.

♪ Mommy/Daddy Paper Plate Mask

VOCABULARY PRACTICE: **MOMMY, DADDY**

DEVELOPMENTAL BENEFITS: problem solving, grasp and hold movements

MATERIALS: two paper plates, tongue depressor, newspaper, stapler, tape, pictures of Mommy and Daddy (optional: clear contact paper)

DIRECTIONS: Tape a tongue depressor "lollipop style" between two paper plates. Stuff the space between the paper plates with newspaper to prevent collapse. Staple the plates together, and cover the staples with tape. Affix a picture of Mommy on one side of the plate and a picture of Daddy on the other side. You can also attach the pictures with clear contact paper to make the toy "drool-proof."

Ask your child if he would like to play with the MOMMY-DADDY toy. Show him one side and ask him to touch DADDY. Repeat for MOMMY. After he has mastered this game, allow him to hold the toy and ask him, "Is that MOMMY or DADDY?" while pointing to one of the pictures.

A SIGN OF SUCCESS

♪ Stimulating Your Baby's Brain

Babies come prewired. Their brains are covered with billions of *neural fibers* ready and waiting for stimulation in the form of interesting and appropriate sensory experiences. Never was the phrase "use it or lose it" more fitting. Howard Gardner, author of *Frames of Mind,* writes, "In human beings, the density of synapses [nerve signals] increases sharply during the first months of life, reaches a maximum at the ages of one to two, declines between the ages of two and sixteen, and remains relatively constant until the age of 72." The *neocortex* is the part of the brain that controls thinking—including reasoning, language, and problem solving—and it can be physiologically altered through experience and learning.

Involvement with music has numerous "brain benefits" for babies and toddlers.

Birth to three years of age is a critically important time for the development of motor, music, and communication skills, as well as social attachment. *Baby Sing & Sign* activities incorporate movement, language, and music and provide a balance of novel and familiar ideas to stimulate the baby's developing brain.

To consider how this development works, think of your infant's brain as a Chia Pet! If it is well tended, this plant will sprout lots of green grass similar to the picture on the product's packaging. Similarly, infants must be given opportunities to focus on interesting activities and try to figure out their meaning so that their "green grass" will grow and flourish. Nerve cells that are not stimulated are systematically pruned from birth to around age ten. This pruning is most pronounced in early childhood.

Parents and caregivers can support their baby's rapidly developing thinking skills by providing an assortment of engaging activities during the child's first years of life. A baby's neurological growth is enhanced by involving all of the senses. His brain is a sensory processor, which makes it possible for him to make sense of the external world. That is why play, language, and music are so beneficial in early childhood—they're sensory practice. *Baby Sing & Sign*'s music and sign language activities require babies to simultaneously look, listen, and move—perfect practice for your baby's growing brain.

In *Nurturing Your Child with Music,* John Ortiz asserts that early music experiences with babies teach them to focus their listening skills and to detect changes in melody, harmony, and rhythm. They understand that the voice can be a musical instrument and begin to sharpen their musical memory skills. Hearing a variety of vocal qualities also helps the child to interpret a person's emotional state, such as happy, sad, or anxious.

Other "brain-friendly" techniques for helping babies think include:

○ Immersing him in interesting, multisensory learning experiences during the course of your daily routine together.

○ Creating learning opportunities that provide a balance of novelty and familiarity so that the child is excited but not overwhelmed or bored by the task.

○ Allowing your baby to problem-solve by actively participating in his learning with a variety of hands-on play materials, games, and songs.

○ Giving many opportunities to practice new skills so that your child begins to understand there is an order and meaningful pattern to all the information he initially perceives as random experience.

○ Understanding that all learning is emotional and that your baby's frustration simply means he is developing persistence and passion for problem solving.

Baby Sing & Sign activities incorporate movement, language, and music and provide a balance of novel and familiar ideas to stimulate the baby's developing brain.

Economist Robert J. Shiller once said, "The ability to focus attention on important things is a defining characteristic of intelligence." This wisdom applies to parent and caregiver as well as baby. What could be more important than our relationship with the children we love and our interest in setting them on the path to learning and discovery?

BOOKS TO READ

I like books that defy probability. The sillier the story, the more I like it. *Daddy Is a Doodle-bug* by Bruce Degen (HarperCollins) meets my criteria perfectly. A father doodlebug and his son like to do the same cool and crazy things together. And fortunately for the reader, many of these things rhyme with "doodle." The resulting verse is great fun to listen to, and the illustrations are rich as well. In addition to DADDY, the book includes these signs: CHAIR and PLAY (chapter 3), DOG (chapter 4), EAT and APPLE (chapter 7), WATER (chapter 11), and BOOK (chapter 12).

MOMMY

Are You My Mother? by P. D. Eastman (Random House Books for Young Readers)

I Love My Mama by Peter Kavanagh (Simon and Schuster)

My Mommy by Matthew Price (Gingham Dog Press)

My Mother Is Mine by Marion Dane Bauer (Simon and Schuster)

What Mommies Do Best by Laura Numeroff (Little Simon)

Where Is Baby's Mommy? by Karen Katz (Little Simon)

DADDY

Daddy and Me by Karen Katz (Little Simon)

Dad Mine! by Dawn Apperley (Little, Brown)

Daddy Kisses by Anne Gutman and George Hallensleben (Chronicle Books)

My Daddy by Matthew Price (Knopf Books for Young Readers)

What Daddies Do Best by Laura Numeroff (Little Simon)

Where Is Baby's Daddy? by Karen Katz (Little Simon)

MOMMY GO 'ROUND THE SUN

WORDS TO LEARN: **CHAIR/SIT, PLAY/TOY**
WORDS TO REVIEW: **MOMMY, DADDY**

Mommy go 'round the sun.	*Sign MOMMY*
Mommy go 'round the moon.	*Sign MOMMY and MOON**
Mommy go 'round	*Sign MOMMY*
the rocking chair	*Sign CHAIR*
Every afternoon.	
Boom!	*Big bounce of child on your lap*
Daddy go 'round the sun.	*Sign DADDY*
Daddy go 'round the moon.	*Sign DADDY*
and MOON*	
Daddy go 'round	*Sign DADDY*
The rocking chair	*Sign CHAIR*
Every afternoon.	
Boom!	*Big bounce on your lap*

*Add **MOON** sign to the performance of this tune after it has been presented chapter 13).

Variations: Replace **MOMMY/DADDY** with **DOG**gie, **CAT** (kitty) (chapter 4), **FISH**ie (chapter 9), or **BUNNY** (chapter 10) after these signs have been presented.

MOMMY GO 'ROUND THE SUN

Mom - my go 'round the sun.
Dad - dy go 'round the sun.

Mom - my go 'round the moon.
Dad - dy go 'round the moon.

Mom - my go 'round the rock - ing chair
Dad - dy go 'round the rock - ing chair

ev - 'ry af - ter - noon. BOOM!
ev - 'ry af - ter - noon. BOOM!

Traditional
Adapted by Anne Meeker Miller

CHAIR/SIT

Form closed two fingers palm-down with both hands. Tap one on top of the other, as if one hand "sits" on the other..

Child may place one flat hand on top of the other.

PLAY/TOY

Hold hands with thumb and pinky extended and middle three fingers folded. Twist both hands side to side at wrist.

Child may shake open fingers with one or two hands.

TIPS FOR INTRODUCING
MOMMY GO 'ROUND THE SUN

○ Ask your child if he would like to PLAY a game with you.

○ Place him on your lap either facing you or facing out. Bend your knees slightly. Bounce the child to the beat depending upon his preference—some like gentle bobbing, while others have a more robust taste in their bouncing. *Be sure to provide adequate security for your toddler by holding him at the waist or hands.*

○ Babies can participate in the bounce if you hold them in your lap or lay them on your arm with their heads resting gently in your hand. This gives them the neck support they need while still allowing them to make eye contact with you.

○ Stop the bounce to sign MOMMY, DADDY, and CHAIR as the words occur in the song. To free your hands for signing, try sliding the child, facing forward, down your thighs so he is perched securely on your upper legs. Babies who have their backs to you can watch you sign in front of them.

○ On the word "boom," you can modify your PLAY by doing any of the following:
  ◆ Give an extra-bouncy bounce
  ◆ "Open the trap doors"—open your legs and allow the child to gently land on the floor in between your legs while holding him at the waist or under the arms
  ◆ Lower your straight legs to the floor
  ◆ Introduce an action of your own creation, such as a tickle or hug

♪ More Musical Fun with *Mommy Go 'Round the Sun*

● Try making the song an activity that involves moving around. Carry your baby or walk with your child to the beat using a bouncy gait.

● Walk around any chair the child chooses: rocking chair, high chair, daddy's chair, grandma's chair, baby's chair. "Fall down" by sitting on the chair or kneeling to the ground when you get to the "boom."

● Invite siblings, other family members, or friends to join you for a "Ring Around the Rosie" version of the song. "All fall down" on "boom."

GAMES TO PLAY

♪ Baby Go in the Car Seat

VOCABULARY PRACTICE: CHAIR/SIT, PLAY/TOY

DEVELOPMENTAL BENEFITS: cooperation, problem solving

MATERIALS: high chair or rocking chair, car seat

DIRECTIONS: Getting children to cooperate while putting them in their car seats is often a challenge. Here is a playful way to approach this task. Sing "[your baby's name] Go 'Round" as you prepare to put the child into the car seat. Time your singing so that you click the latch shut on "boom." The synchronization of the click and "boom" is fun for baby and is a good experience in predicting auditory events for your baby's developing brain.

Children who are able (and eager!) to climb into their own car seats on their own can play the same game. You may need to speed up or slow down your singing in order to make the click and "boom" come out just right. That can be part of the fun of the game. If your child is very speedy in climbing in and turning around, you will need to sing very quickly. This will appeal to your child's developing sense of humor.

Turn power struggles into **PLAY** with a musical car seat game.

♪ Nesting Cans

VOCABULARY PRACTICE: **PLAY/TOY, MORE, ALL-DONE**

DEVELOPMENTAL BENEFITS: problem solving, relationships in space, ability to manipulate objects

MATERIALS: tin cans of various sizes, contact paper, cloth tape

DIRECTIONS: Collect several empty tin cans of various diameters (one-pound coffee can, fruit, soup, tomato paste, etc.). Completely remove one end of each can. Hammer down any place where metal sticks out on the inside rim. Soak off labels. Cover the cans with brightly colored contact paper. Cover rims with cloth tape. Your toddler can stack or nest the cans.

Ask your child if she wants to PLAY with the TOY cans. Allow her to stack or nest the cans. If she knocks down a can tower, sign ALL-DONE? Then ask her if she wants MORE and start the game again.

By playing with toys like the nesting cans,
children learn that toys do not have to come from a toy store.

A SIGN OF SUCCESS

♪ BUSY BABIES CALM DOWN ♪

Inchworm, inchworm
Measuring the marigolds
Seems to me you'd stop and see
How beautiful they are.
—Lyrics by Frank Loesser
(Featured in the movie *Hans Christian Andersen*)

Have you ever noticed how some babies never stop moving? They are busy, busy, busy people all day long. If you have a busy motor baby in your home, the thought of him slowing down long enough to absorb the signs you want to teach him may appear hopelessly optimistic.

Sarah's two-year-old son, Eric, was a busy motor baby. Calling him active "but not out of control," Sarah wasn't sure what to expect when they first joined a Baby Sing & Sign class when Eric was ten months old. "He actually loved it," Sarah explained. "I felt it was a good experience for him." Eric was a crawler and constantly on the go, but his mother found he was still tuning in to what was happening around him. "Once the singing started, he would crawl right back," she said. "He was mesmerized by the music."

Music can be an effective way to bring busy motor babies back to a span of attention. Many studies have demonstrated the profound effect music can have on the intelligence and behavior of babies. The intensity of an infant's attention to sensory stimuli such as music varies greatly from child to child. Some children respond better to familiar and repeated routines or experiences. Other children more readily focus attention on what's new and different in their world.

Mom and Lucy are making music on the move!

"Babies come into the world prepared to enjoy what is novel as well as what is familiar. They pay more focused and intense attention to new stimuli, especially those coming from the human world," wrote Lois Barclay Murphy, PhD, and Rachel Moon, MD. One way to coax attention from your busy motor baby is to continually bring him new and exciting discoveries. The descriptions of the added benefits of the handmade toys and games throughout this book may prove helpful in providing the new stimuli necessary to keep your child focused on learning the signs.

Though boys tend to fall into that busy motor baby category more often than girls, there are many busy baby girls in the world today, too. Heather participated with her daughter, Taylor, in a Baby Sing & Sign class just before Taylor's first birthday. Heather describes her daughter as someone who enjoys fully immersing herself in the sensory experiences presented to her. "She wants to feel it, touch it, experience it with you," Heather explained. "She's curious." Taylor enjoyed the class and was especially enthralled by the class leader's guitar and the silliness that often spontaneously broke out.

> Some children respond better to familiar and repeated routines or experiences. Other children more readily focus attention on what's new and different in their world.

Taylor took to signing words well, regularly using PLEASE, MORE, EAT, DRINK, DOG, CAT, and FISH. Taylor's parents coped with her tendency to be busily preoccupied by always taking their cues from her when it came to practicing the signs. "When we're at home, I take my cues from her. We do as much as she wants to do," Heather said. Even though she was speaking two-word sentences by eighteen months of age, Taylor continues using her signs. "Sometimes when she gets frustrated or she can't get her point across, she'll revert to signing," Heather said.

Logan is twenty-two months old and his mother's fourth and last child. Lyn was already well versed in American Sign Language and had taught her older children to sign on her own. Lyn saw the *Baby Sing & Sign* class as a way to indulge Logan with some special "just Mommy and me" time as well as offering her a final chance to do something fun with a baby. "The class looked fun and a good follow-up to what I had already done," Lyn explained. Logan enjoyed the chance to have some interactive fun with all the homemade toys and activities, and he really liked the class leader, seeking out and engaging her frequently during the class. At home, Logan's older siblings helped him with his signs, and according to Lyn, getting attention from them became "total positive reinforcement" for what was being taught in class. Logan indicates how much he wants what he's asking for by how emphatically he signs. "He signs with great passion when he really wants something," his mother noted.

According to Murphy and Moon, babies learn about the world either through active exploration or quiet observation. Busy motor babies earn that title because they are the active explorers. And though it may require some extra effort to hold their attention, the benefits of better communication between parent and child make such efforts extremely worthwhile.

BOOKS TO READ

It will probably come as no surprise to you that I like to sing stories. When a picture book has rhythm, rhyme, and repetition, it is a prime candidate for adding a tune to tell the tale. I usually borrow one from a familiar song. When I sing the story, I can play with the continuum of sound while I warble—both high and low, loud and soft, fast and slow. These artistic liberties enhance the engagement for my "book lookers" and increase the likelihood that my baby friends will want to read the same book with me again. One of my favorite books to sing is *Jesse Bear, What Will You Wear?* by Nancy White Carlstrom and Bruce Degen (Little Simon). The tune choice is always up to the reader, but I would mention that "Here We Go 'Round the Mulberry Bush" fits perfectly with the lilt of this lovely story. Jesse gets stuck in his seat, so be ready to laugh out loud when he "wears his CHAIR!"

CHAIR/SIT

Miss Spider's Tea Party by David Kirk (Callaway and Kirk)
My Chair by Betsy James (Arthur A. Levine)
Peter's Chair by Ezra Jack Keats (Viking Juvenile)
The Chair Where Bear Sits by Lee Wardlaw and Russell Benfanti (Winslow Press)
The Three Bears by Paul Galdone (Clarion Books)

PLAY/TOY

Corduroy's Toys by Don Freeman (Viking Press)
Hey, Look at Me! I Like to Play (Book for Boys) by Merry Fleming Thomasson (Merrybooks, and More)
Hey, Look at Me! I Like to Play (Book for Girls) by Merry Fleming Thomasson (Merrybooks, and More)
Max's Toys by Rosemary Wells (Viking Books)
Play with Me by Marie Hall Ets (Penguin Books)
Tub Toys by Terry Miller Shannon and Lee Calderon (Tricycle Press)

4

DOGGIE, DOGGIE

WORDS TO LEARN: **DOG, CAT, BALL**
WORD TO REVIEW: **PLAY/TOY**

Doggie, Doggie,	*Sign DOG*
Who has your ball?	*Sign BALL*
Doggie, Doggie,	*Sign DOG*
Who has your ball?	*Sign BALL*
Doggie, Doggie,	*Sign DOG*
Who has your ball?	*Sign BALL*
Doggie, Doggie,	*Sign DOG*
Who has your ball?	*Sign BALL*
Kitty cat, Kitty cat,	*Sign CAT*
Who has your toy?	*Sign TOY*
Kitty cat, Kitty cat,	*Sign CAT*
Who has your toy?	*Sign TOY*
Kitty cat, Kitty cat,	*Sign CAT*
Who has your toy?	*Sign TOY*
Kitty cat, Kitty cat,	*Sign CAT*
Who has your toy?	*Sign TOY*
Baby, who has your book?	*Sign BOOK**
Baby, who has your book?	*Sign BOOK*
Baby, who has your book?	*Sign BOOK*
Baby, who has your book?	*Sign BOOK*

*Add **BOOK** sign to the performance of this tune after it has been presented (chapter 12)

DOGGIE, DOGGIE

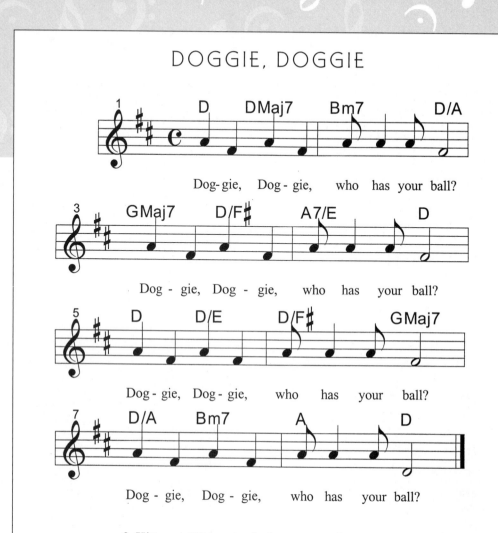

Dog-gie, Dog-gie, who has your ball?

Dog-gie, Dog-gie, who has your ball?

Dog-gie, Dog-gie, who has your ball?

Dog-gie, Dog-gie, who has your ball?

2. Kitty cat, Kitty cat, who has your toy?
   Kitty cat...

3. (Your child's name), (your child's name),
   who has your book?

By Anne Meeker Miller

DOG

Pat your side several times as if
calling a dog.

CAT

Draw pinched thumb and pointer away
from cheek, representing the cat's whiskers.

BALL

Bring hands together to form shape of ball
with *open fingers*.

Child may clap hands in up and down
direction.

TIPS FOR INTRODUCING *DOGGIE, DOGGIE*

○ This song has a very simple tune. Only three pitches are used in the melody. The descending pattern is the essence of this song, which children sing naturally all over the world. The simplicity and repetition of the song enhance the opportunity to practice baby sign.

○ Place your child on your lap facing you or facing out. Sing the song using a moderate tempo, and sign DOG, BALL, CAT, and TOY as they occur in the lyrics.

♪ More Musical Fun with *Doggie, Doggie*

ITEMS NEEDED: small ball, toy, medium-sized stuffed toy dog and cat

● Find a small BALL and TOY, such as a rattle, that baby can hold comfortably in her hand. You will also need DOG and CAT stuffed animals large enough to cover the small BALL and TOY.

● Hide the ball under the stuffed DOG. Sing the song and pantomime the question "Who has your BALL?" by raising your eyebrows and looking around for the BALL.

● See if the child will get the BALL from beneath the DOG. If the child does not initiate this action, help her find the BALL by lifting the stuffed DOG.

● Ask if the child would like to repeat the game by signing MORE. Play the game again, but now hide the TOY beneath the stuffed CAT.

Opportunities for focused listening and looking are great for developing a child's attention span.

GAMES TO PLAY

♪ Sock Puppet Pet

VOCABULARY PRACTICE: **DOG, CAT, BALL, TOY**

DEVELOPMENTAL BENEFITS: receptive language, introduction of two-sign phrases

MATERIALS: sock, felt scraps, pipe cleaners or garbage bag twist ties, markers, craft glue (or glue gun if available); for a puppet with an opening mouth, you will also need a piece of lightweight cardboard and needle and thread

DIRECTIONS: Cut felt scraps in the shapes of the eyes, nose, and ears of a cat and dog as shown in the photograph below. Cut pipe cleaners or garbage bag twist ties for the cat's whiskers. You can also add felt spots to the dog. Put your hand into the sock so that your fingers and thumb are in the toe to determine the best placement for the various pieces. Glue or sew them into place.

You can also make the pet's mouth open by following these steps (see picture at right):

1. Cut a slit in the sock.
2. Cut an oval measuring three by five inches out of cardboard.
3. Using this cardboard oval as a pattern, cut a piece of felt approximately one-half inch larger.
4. Glue the cardboard to the felt oval, and fold both in half the short way.
5. Turn the sock inside out.
6. Put the folded oval into your sock by placing right sides together, with the felt side of the oval against the outside cut edge of the sock.
7. Stitch the felt piece into the sock using a running stitch.
8. Turn the puppet inside out.
9. Glue a felt tongue into the mouth along the fold inside its mouth.

You are ready to play! Start with only the DOG puppet. Give your child the small BALL and TOY. Sing the song and finish by saying and signing: *Give DOGgie the BALL.* See if the child will give the ball to the DOG puppet. Now play the game singing the CAT verse. Sing and sign: *Give CAT the TOY.* If your child enjoys the game after many repetitions, she may want to play when you have both puppets on your hands. Most toddlers can differentiate between CAT and DOG and provide the item requested.

LEARNING ABOUT PETS

Signs must have meaning for children if they are to use them in expressive communication with you. If you have a real, live version of a DOG or CAT, these signs will most likely be among the first you will observe your child using in her sign language conversation with you. Do not be offended if CAT and DOG appear long before MOMMY and DADDY.

NOTE: Please do not use a live dog or cat in any of the games presented here. The same wonderful manual dexterity that your child will demonstrate in communicating through gesture can be an irritant for pets—especially when those little fingers end up too close to the animal's ears or eyes. No animals were harmed during the writing of this book.

DOG will likely be one of your child's first signs if you own (and love) one.

A SIGN OF SUCCESS

♪ BEING PATIENT WITH SIGNING ♪

Every really new idea looks crazy at first.
—ALFRED NORTH WHITEHEAD (1861-1947)

Melinda began taking her daughter, Hannah, to *Baby Sing & Sign* class when she was six months old. Gung ho about the concept and the class, Melinda was faithful in practicing the signs with Hannah and playing the music CD every day. She also taught the rest of the family how to sign for Hannah. When Hannah reached ten months and still showed no inclination to sign back, Melinda got discouraged. Burned out and admittedly tired of doing it, she discontinued signing with the exception of two words: MORE and ALL-DONE.

Repetition is essential for baby to learn sign language.

Several weeks later, Melinda was bathing Hannah in the tub while her daughter played with tub toys. All of a sudden, much to Melinda's amazement and joy, Hannah signed the word FISH while reaching for a plastic fish. "You cannot imagine how excited we were," she said. At twelve months, with Melinda enthusiastic about signing again, Hannah started using the signs for MORE and ALL-DONE. She then rapidly progressed to use about ten more signs.

They say patience is a virtue, but it's hard to stay virtuous when you are the parent of an infant or toddler. Busy, hectic lives can interfere, and in a world where instant gratification has become the norm, it can be difficult to "stay the course."

Cathy was another mother who was excited by the prospect of teaching her daughter to sign. They enrolled in *Baby Sing & Sign* class when Heather was seven months old. The music was an immediate hit, but months and months went by with Heather doing no signing at all. Cathy eventually lost interest and continued to do only a few signs on a regular basis, mostly during mealtime. At fourteen months, Heather did her first sign, MORE. She had been drinking a cup of water and had run out. Her mother signed and asked if she wanted more. The toddler watched her mom do the sign three times, then looked up at her mother's face and signed MORE back. But even as Cathy jumped up quickly to refill the cup with water and return it to her child, Heather showed no interest in drinking.

Still, Cathy knew she was demonstrating to Heather that the signs they were practicing had meaning.

They say patience is its own reward, but for most parents the reward comes with the realization that all their efforts have "paid off" and they can now enjoy engaging in true communication with their child. When you are feeling discouraged and wondering if your pantomiming will ever pay off, take inspiration from the magnificent being you are hoping to teach. When your baby learned to crawl, how long did he rock back and forth on all fours before he finally went in forward motion? How many weeks did your child have to cruise the furniture before he let go and took his steps unaided? No true accomplishment happens overnight.

As in the famous joke, "How do you get to Carnegie Hall?" (Practice! Practice!), it sometimes takes patience, patience, and more patience to get your little star performer to sign.

> Take inspiration from the magnificent being you are hoping to teach. No true accomplishment happens overnight.

BOOKS TO READ

I have the same sense of humor as most toddlers. Perhaps that is why I believe *Bark, George* by Jules Feiffer (HarperCollins) is one of the funniest books ever written. George won't bark; he prefers to produce the sounds of other animals instead. There is plenty of repetition and ample opportunity to practice MOTHER and DOG. Whenever you read the word "George," sign DOG. Baby would also love to hear you use a different vocal quality when you read MOTHER's part—perhaps something quite "sing-songy" and dramatic. Even toddlers will get the joke on the last page!

DOG

Bingo by Rosemary Wells (Scholastic)

Doggies: A Counting and Barking Book by Sandra Boynton (Little Simon)

Dog's Noisy Day by Emma Dodd (Dutton Books)

Go, Dog, Go! by P. D. Eastman (Random House Books for Young Readers)

Good Dog, Carl by Alexandra Day (Little Simon)

Harry the Dirty Dog by Gene Zioin (Harper Collins)

CAT

Five Little Kittens by Nancy Jewell and Elizabeth Sayles (Scholastic)

Have You Seen My Cat? by Eric Carle (Aladdin Library)

Kitten's First Full Moon by Kevin Henkes (Greenwillow Books)

Mama Cat Has Three Kittens by Denise Fleming (Henry Holt)

Where Is Little Black Kitten? by Virginia Miller (Candlewick Press)

BALL

Balls! (Elmo's World) by John E. Barrett (Random House for Young Readers)

Bear, and Ball by Cliff Wright (Chronicle Books)

Play Ball by Mercer Mayer (McGraw-Hill Children's Publishers)

Sam's Ball by Barbro Lindgren (William Morrow)

Take Me out to the Ballgame by Jack Norworth (Aladdin Library)

The Story of the Red Rubber Ball by Constance Kling Levy and Hiroe Nakata (Silver Whistle)

5

ROLL THE BALL

WORDS TO LEARN: WANT, PLEASE, HELP, SORRY
WORDS TO REVIEW: BALL, DOG, CAT, MOMMY, DADDY

I roll the ball to [child's name],
he rolls the ball to me.

*Sign BALL and roll ball to your child
Help or encourage your child to roll
the ball back to you*

I roll the ball to [child's name],
he rolls the ball to me.

*Sign BALL and roll ball to your child
Help or encourage your child to roll
the ball back to you*

Roll the ball, roll the ball,
roll the ball, roll the ball,

Sway side to side as you sign BALL

I roll the ball to [child's name],
He rolls the ball to me.

*Sign BALL and roll ball to your child
Help or encourage your child to roll
the ball back to you*

ROLL THE BALL

2. I roll the ball to mommy...
3. I roll the ball to doggie...
4. I roll the ball to kitty cat...

"Roll the Ball" from *The Book of Simple Songs and Circles* by John M. Feierabend
Copyright © 1996 by GIA Publications, Inc., Chicago, Illinois
All rights reserved.
Adapted with permission by Anne Meeker Miller

WANT

PLEASE

Pull *open fingers* toward body one time with palms up and fingertips slightly curved, as if drawing something desirable toward you.

Rub *open fingers* on upper chest in circular motion.

TIPS FOR INTRODUCING *ROLL THE BALL*

○ This song is destined to be your child's favorite. (You do not need to tell the child that he is developing important motor skills as well as language and musical skills while doing it!)

○ Sit your child on the floor facing you. Help him sit with his legs in a "V" position on the floor so you can easily roll a ball to him. Make sure your child is making eye contact with you so that he is prepared to receive the ball!

○ Gently roll the BALL to your baby, and see if he will push the BALL back to you. Babies are most successful with medium-sized, light BALLS, such as an inflatable beach BALL. Toddlers enjoy a variety of BALLS. Try BALLS of different sizes and textures.

○ Roll the BALL on the lyric "roll." Sing that word slightly louder, giving it the proper emphasis for an action word. Your child may learn to perform the rolling action on cue when it is his turn to roll the BALL to you. Lean side to side on "Roll the BALL, roll the BALL," and then continue the BALL rolling on the last line of the song. See if your child will imitate your rhythmic leaning. He may move his head or rock from side to side.

○ Be sure to give your child plenty of time to respond to the game. If necessary, provide a verbal prompt such as "your turn" or "roll the BALL to MOMMY!" Make sure to sing "roll" at the exact moment the child pushes the BALL.

○ This is a favorite song of most children!

♪ More Musical Fun with *Roll the Ball*

ITEMS NEEDED: balls of different dimensions, weights, and textures

- This song gives you another opportunity to practice MORE. When time permits, allow your baby to repeat the game until it is her idea to be finished and ready for a new game. Combine signs into a short phrase by asking her if she wants MORE BALL.

- Be sure to use BALLS of different dimensions, weights, and textures. Your baby must learn that BALLS come in all shapes and sizes. The ability to apply one label to several specific items is called "generalization."

- Play or sing the song for your child. Hide a ball behind your back, and ask your baby what she WANTS. If she signs BALL, PLAY, or MORE, start the "Roll the Ball" game immediately. If she does not sign in response, start playing the "Roll the Ball" game anyway. There is no keeping score in this ball game!

- Children often begin using the sign PLEASE interchangeably with MORE once it is introduced. It is never too early to introduce manners! Ask your child if she would like to play ball. Sign PLEASE for her and say, "Tell me PLEASE." You can also help her make the sign and praise her for her good "talking."

- Ask your baby if she will HELP you with a BALL game. Ask her to HELP you with other tasks that will appeal to her. Begin to also use the HELP word in situations where she appears frustrated or could use your assistance. Praise her for asking for HELP by "using her words." Allowing your child to choose to ask for HELP goes a long way toward preserving her dignity while giving her the support she needs to master new skills.

HELP

Place *closed fist* on other *flat hand* and lift both, as if "helping" to raise the *closed fist*.

Child may cover one hand with the other and lift both.

LEARNING MANNERS WITH SIGNS

♪ Love Means *Always* Saying You're SORRY

Children do not come with manners and civility already installed. Some assembly on your part is required. Focusing on manners from the start through signing will help your child begin to master this essential life lesson. Model your best manners in relationships with others as well as with your child. It is important that you convey the *idea* of how we behave toward one another and add the specifics as life experiences present themselves. Modeling good manners is the best way to teach a child to be polite. Start with basic words, such as PLEASE, THANK YOU (chapter 9), and SORRY, as soon as your child begins to use signed or spoken words to communicate.

Children also need opportunities to practice their manners with children their own age. Schedule play dates so that your youngster can learn to share her space—and stuff—with others. It is important to establish some ground rules for child play. Although toddlers are not developmentally ready to share their favorite toys with others, parents can help direct playmates in taking turns. Parental praise also goes a long way in encouraging "playing nice." Tell your child, "I like the way you let Tommy play with your blocks."

And, of course, there is the time-honored verbal prompt "What do you say?" with the expectation that your child will learn which word is called for—PLEASE, SORRY, or

THANK YOU—and will ultimately express these words without you nearby. The best of parents find themselves persisting with this prompt long after the toddler years are over. However, the journey in pursuit of good manners will be much smoother if you start early!

SORRY

Rub *closed fist* on upper chest in circular motion.

GAMES TO PLAY

♪ Having a Ball with Your Baby

VOCABULARY PRACTICE: BALL
DEVELOPMENTAL BENEFITS: balance, sensory experience
MATERIALS: exercise ball or other large ball

DIRECTIONS: Perhaps you purchased an exercise ball in an attempt to return your waistline to its trim pre-maternity measurement. Now you can use it to exercise your arm muscles as well with the assistance of your child. *Babies need good head control in order to play this game.* Put the exercise ball in between your legs, or kneel and place the ball in front of you. Place your child on top of the ball—holding him around the rib cage or under the arms—and move him in a circular fashion on the lyric "Roll."

The "rolling" movement shifts the fluid in the inner ear, which influences children's sensation of posture and balance. Modify the rolling movement of the song based on your child's age and preference. Some children (and adults) like the feeling of being out of balance, while others prefer staying closer to their center.

"When my daughter was six to seven weeks, I would lay her with her tummy on the exercise ball and gently roll her from side to side and forward and back while supporting her back. I did that as a way to incorporate 'tummy time' but also to begin strengthening her neck muscles. We sang while we gently rolled. When she was able to sit up, we switched to gentle upright bouncing. We used it with your 'Roll the Ball' song. It was a big hit at our house!"

—Amy

♪ Hose Balls

VOCABULARY PRACTICE: **BALL, PLAY, MOMMY, DADDY**
DEVELOPMENTAL BENEFITS: improve child's ability to reach, grasp, hold, and throw
MATERIALS: pair of panty hose, fiberfill, scissors, jingle bell (optional)

DIRECTIONS: Cut a section of the leg from a pair of panty hose and knot one end. Turn inside out and fill with fiberfill to the desired size. Knot the other end. You can wrap a jingle bell inside the fiberfill to make a musical ball.

This ball is easy for young children to manipulate because it is soft and therefore simpler to grasp. Ask your child if he wants to PLAY BALL. Direct him to throw the ball to MOMMY or DADDY. Ask him to "tell me with your hands" who has the ball—MOMMY or DADDY?

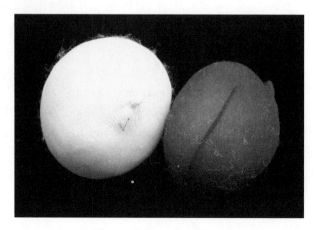

A SIGN OF SUCCESS

♪ YOUR CHILD DESIRES TO MAKE CHOICES ♪

The world is so full of a number of things,
I'm sure we should all be as happy as kings.
—ROBERT LOUIS STEVENSON

The vast majority of expectant parents I know spend hundreds of hours and a great portion of their disposable income preparing the perfect nursery. They fill this special little room with all the things they believe their baby will want and need in the months to come. Family members and friends add more toys and gadgets, often with reassuring recommendations such as "This was Buster's favorite toy" or "When Miguel was little, we couldn't have managed without this fabulous thingamajig."

And then Baby arrives. For a while he will agree that for the most part you are doing a splendid job meeting his constant and varied requirements for happiness. In your clairvoyant, albeit sleep-deprived, way you are giv-

So many balls to choose from: red, yellow, green, or blue?

ing it the "old college try," and your baby thanks you. However, much like the teenager who finds his parents growing more stupid with each passing year (until he grows up and becomes a parent himself), your baby's passage from infancy to toddlerhood will morph from idyllic love fest to something more closely resembling a food fight. When your child is old enough to throw food at you with passion and purpose, you will know you have truly crossed over.

So where did you go wrong? Did you fail to assemble the "right stuff?" Is there a toy or device requisite for good parenting that you somehow overlooked?

The good news is that your toddler's escalating angst is what we call "developmentally appropriate," and has more to do with how he gets what he wants than the object—toy, cracker, power tool—he actually desires. What novice parents rarely understand is that the inner struggle for control begins in infancy, and that what you may consider an abject failure in parenting is in fact an indicator that your child will ultimately be an independent and responsible citizen.

However, as with most good things, there is a catch. Babies need caring adults to give them just the right amount of control over the decisions in their lives. Foster Cline, MD, and Jim Fay, authors of *Parenting with Love and Logic,* suggest that as parents we allow our children to take as much control as possible, "always cutting our kids in on the action."

> Babies need caring adults to give them just the right amount of control over the decisions in their lives.

It is good, right, and natural that your child wants to think for himself. The key is to make choices available within a consistent framework of limits. Allowing a young child too much control undermines the benefit of developing independence and creates what is commonly referred to as a "spoiled brat." And trust me—you do not want one of those. Psychologist Sylvia B. Rimm, PhD, cautions that it is far easier to allow more choices as the child grows older than to take away choices that the child has already enjoyed.

What are some decisions that a toddler can make? Here are a few suggestions:

- Green beans or carrots?
- Blocks or puzzle?
- *Goodnight Moon* or *The Runaway Bunny?*
- "Doggie, Doggie" or "Mommy Go 'Round the Sun"?

One of the wonders of sign language is that it enables preverbal children to express their wants and needs and then make the choices that satisfy their quest for autonomy and control. Make sure you allow your child to utilize his emerging ability to communicate by giving him appropriate opportunities to decide what will happen next.

BOOKS TO READ

Bears awaking from a long winter of hibernation are hungry and WANT to EAT. *Bear Wants More* by Karma Wilson and Jane Chapman (Margaret K. McElderry Books) is the story of one such bear and his snacking adventures with many helpful animal friends. Much like a hungry toddler, this gluttonous bear WANTS MORE and MORE FOOD. You will have many opportunities to practice signs for WANT and MORE all the way to the happy ending.

WANT

Do You Want to Be My Friend? by Eric Carle (HarperFestival)

How Many Kisses Do You Want Tonight? by Vasha Bajaj (Little, Brown)

The Little Red Hen by Paul Galdone (Clarion Books)

What Baby Wants by Phyllis Root and Jill Barton (Candlewick Press)

PLEASE

Brush Your Teeth Please by Eric Carle (Simon and Schuster)

Chicken Fingers, Mac and Cheese . . . Why Do You Always Have to Say Please? by Wendy Rosen
(Modern Publishing)

Excuse Me! A Little Book of Manners by Karen Katz (Grosset and Dunlap)

Richard Scarry's Please and Thank You Book by Richard Scarry (Random House for Young Readers)

Time to Say "Please" by Mo Willems (Hyperion Books)

Toby's Please and Thank You by Cyndy Szekeres (Little Simon)

HELP

Help! by Christopher Inns (Frances Lincoln)

Herman the Helper by Robert Kraus (Aladdin Books)

Honey Helps by Laura Godwin and Jane Chapman (Aladdin Paperbacks)

Lucy Wants to Help by Thea Ross (Parklane Publishing)

With a Little Help from Daddy by Dan Andreasen (Simon and Schuster)

SORRY

David Gets in Trouble by David Shannon (Scholastic)

Samuel, lo siento / Sorry Sam by Nicholas Turpin and Barbara Nascimbeni (Gingham Dog Press)

Oops by David Shannon (Scholastic)

Oops, Sorry! A First Book of Manners by Richard Morgan (Barron's Educational Series)

OH, DAVID! by David Shannon (Scholastic)

THE WALKING SONG

WORDS TO LEARN: **STOP, ALL-DONE, OUCH/HURT, HOT**
WORDS TO REVIEW: **MORE, WANT, PLEASE, PLAY/TOY**

Walking, walking, walking, walking.

Walk holding child or next to child while holding her hand

Walking, walking, now let's stop.

Stop walking, then sing and sign STOP

Walking, walking, walking, walking.

Walk holding child or next to child while holding her hand

Walking, walking, now let's stop.

Stop walking, then sing and sign STOP

Verse 2. Hopping . . .

Repeat circle game, but "hop" by shifting weight from foot to foot while moving forward.

Verse 3. Running . . .

Repeat circle game, but "run" by moving feet quickly and moving forward at a moderate pace (no racing necessary!).

Verse 4. Playing [music or toys]

Help your child play instruments and stop playing when you sing and sign STOP.

THE WALKING SONG

Walk- ing, walk- ing, walk- ing, walk- ing.

Walk - ing, walk - ing, now let's stop.

Walk - ing, walk - ing, walk - ing, walk - ing.

Walk - ing, walk - ing, now let's stop.

2. Hopping...
3. Running...
4. Playing (music or toys)...

Sung to the tune of "Sourwood Mountain"
Traditional
Adapted by Anne Meeker Miller

STOP

Move little-finger side of one hand
abruptly onto open palm of other hand
in a single chopping motion.

TIPS FOR INTRODUCING *THE WALKING SONG*

○ Depending on the age of your child, you can either hold her or walk with her in this activity. An older child might enjoy your singing while she performs the actions "solo."

○ Walk to the beat of the song and stop in an exaggerated fashion on the word STOP. If you have a free hand or are very talented, you may be able to sign STOP while carrying your child.

○ At the conclusion of the song, sign ALL-DONE and tell the child, "Good STOP." Ask her if she would like to sing the song again by signing MORE?

○ Repeat for the other actions in the song. If you are carrying the child, your "hop" can consist of shifting your weight from foot to foot, which causes the child to bounce in your arms. Feeling the rhythmic accent of the bounces is great musical stimulation. The same is true for the "run" action. The faster running bounce is great fun!

ALL-DONE

Hold *open fingers* in front of you with palms toward your chest. Flip hands to palms facing out.

♪ More Musical Fun with *The Walking Song*

- STOP, ALL-DONE, PLEASE, and MORE can be incorporated into most songs. When you finish a song, sign STOP or ALL-DONE. Ask your child if she wants MORE. She can respond with MORE or PLEASE. When you begin to observe the child using single signs to express her wants and needs, you might want to try to introduce two-sign phrases such as MORE PLEASE or WANT MORE.

- You can also make a game of interrupting your singing by signing STOP. You can then sign and ask, "MORE?" Wait for the child to sign MORE, or prompt her by helping her sign the word. Tell her, "Good signing MORE!" Then continue singing or playing the music CD. Use the same technique with other signs, such as PLEASE and WANT.

- Try singing the song without the musical recording so that you can make the STOP intervals longer and sillier.

- This is a wonderful song to use when transitioning between playtime, meals, and naptime.

- Play "Follow the Leader" at home, at the park, or out on a walk while singing the song. Older children will want to take a turn as leader.

- Make up new verses for daily activities such as eating, washing, playing, or putting away toys.

LEARNING ABOUT SAFETY

Hannah and her mother spend time together every day walking to the mailbox and singing "The Walking Song." Hannah anticipates the STOP direction in the song by stopping slightly before her mother sings the STOP lyric. Several months after they had started this ritual, Hannah and her mother were shopping at a crowded mall. The little girl managed to get away from her mother and continued running away. As she glanced over her shoulder, she saw her mother sign STOP and immediately halted. This gave her mother the time she needed to catch up to Hannah and retrieve her safely. Signing can be a powerful tool for communicating what is essential to keep your child out of harm's way.

Signing can also help your child communicate pain or discomfort. If you sense your child has injured himself or is not feeling well, sign HURT and ask him where he HURTS. Touch various parts of his body and ask him to use his fingers to tell where it HURTS.

Another sign that is helpful for avoiding injury is HOT. This may be used in reference to fire, stoves, radiators, or cooked foods. Bobby uses his HOT sign to ask whether a food is too hot to eat every time he is given a dish of FOOD. Although it can be comical to observe him sign HOT with an inquiring look on his face when he is given a dish of ice cream, his caution is appreciated and acknowledged by his parents.

OUCH/HURT

Both pointers repeatedly move toward each other at the location of the pain.

Child may move fists toward center or point with one hand to location of pain.

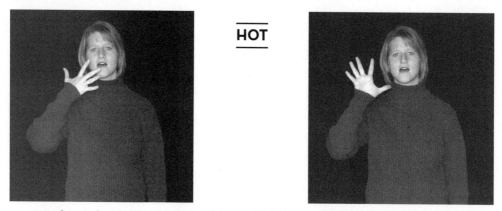

HOT

Open fingers of one hand, touch chin, and then quickly flick out to show that the food is too hot to eat.
Can be paired with an "H" sound or blowing.

GAMES TO PLAY

♪ Sound Toys

VOCABULARY PRACTICE: MUSIC, STOP

DEVELOPMENTAL BENEFITS: reach, grasp and hold movements, listening skills, eye-hand coordination

MATERIALS: empty containers (Tic Tac box, film canister, plastic Easter eggs), dried rice, popcorn kernels, electrical tape

DIRECTIONS: Make a variety of sound toys for children to handle and listen to. Try an empty Tic Tac box, a 35-mm film canister, a candy bon-bon tin, or plastic Easter eggs with dried rice or popcorn kernels inside. Be certain the lids are taped on securely to keep tops and contents out of the child's mouth. Electrical tape can be purchased in primary colors from your local hardware store and is good for securing the closures on your sound toys.

These sound toys are great accompaniments to the "playing" verse of "The Walking Song." Sing along with your child and see if she will STOP as directed. Children can improvise their own accompaniment to any tune they choose.

♪ Baby's Kitchen Band

VOCABULARY: PLAY, STOP, MUSIC

DEVELOPMENTAL BENEFITS: reach and grasp movements, eye-hand coordination

MATERIALS: pots and pans, kitchen utensils

DIRECTIONS: Introduce your child to the joy of playing pots and pans in the kitchen. Use kitchen items with a variety of surface types, such as metal and wood, to experience different sound qualities. *Be sure that you are close at hand to monitor your child's safety.* Have your child move her hands to shorten the length of the wooden spoon or spatula used as drumsticks. This will help prevent her from inadvertently whacking herself. Tell the child that you like to listen to her make MUSIC.

After the child has had an opportunity to explore, you can structure sign practice by singing the PLAYING verse of "The Walking Song." Gently place your hands over your child's when you sing STOP, thus preventing her from playing the kitchen MUSIC. Alter the duration of your STOP intervals from just a few seconds to several seconds. Observe carefully how your child tolerates these little episodes of frustration. Does she learn to anticipate where STOP occurs in the song?

Gilli PLAYS the pots and pans with great enthusiasm!

A SIGN OF SUCCESS

♪ HELPING YOUR CHILD'S CAREGIVERS LEARN TO SIGN ♪

It takes a village to raise a child.
—OLD AFRICAN PROVERB

From the moment a baby awakens in the morning until she drifts off to sleep for the last time at night, she is under the watchful eye of a caregiver. That caregiver is often a parent, but in a society where more and more families have two breadwinners, many babies spend at least a portion of their day in the care of a nonfamily member. Whether the caregiver is a nanny who comes into your home for one-on-one care; an off-site, in-home day-care provider; or professionals employed by a commercial day-care facility, at the end of the day your child will have spent time being influenced and guided by others.

In the best of circumstances, a child's caregivers and parents share the same values and work together as a team to ensure consistency in the child's care and upbringing. Communication is as important between parent and caregiver as it is between parent and child, as well as between caregiver and child. Therefore, babies who are being taught sign language benefit most when both parents and caregivers participate.

Megan is a preschool teacher working at a child and family development center on an urban college campus. Megan uses *Baby Sing & Sign*'s companion CD during daily group time not only because it facilitates the teaching of the signs but also because her charges love the music in and of itself. She has started teaching her infants and toddlers signs that deal with food and mealtime, such as MORE, WATER, and ALL-DONE. "The kids are really happy when they sign MORE and WATER and—bam!—their needs are met," Megan said. "Even the kids who aren't signing yet are beginning to know what it means." Her center employs advanced technology to document the activities of each child each day. Parents are informed by e-mails of what new things their child has learned. If a child starts making a sign, it is noted on the daily e-mail. That way, parents can ask about the sign the next time they are in the classroom and can choose to reinforce it by demonstrating the same sign at home.

> Babies who are being taught sign language benefit most when both parents and caregivers participate.

Danielle is a former teacher who for two years has operated an in-home daycare for six children, including two of her own. She has taught the children sign language and has found it helpful in easing children's frustration. In addition to the meal-centered words MORE, ALL-DONE, DRINK, and EAT, Danielle has trained her charges to use SORRY and THANK YOU with one another as well as with her. "They're very good about signing I'm SORRY to each other," she said. "The kids love the songs and enjoy listening to the CD every day." When a child has mastered a new sign, she will also use it at home, which prompts the parent to inquire the next day about the sign's meaning. "I answer their questions and teach the parents the signs as well," she said. "I have wonderful parents who understand that anything I do with their children has to be done in partnership with them."

While a parent is always a child's first and best teacher, it's important to remember that the village that helps rear her has many fine teachers, too.

Margaret shares signs, songs, and snuggles with the child she cares for.

BOOKS TO READ

Sandra Boynton is one woman who is in touch with her "inner toddler." My favorite in her considerable collection is a book and recording set called *Rhinoceros Tap* (Workman). Boynton brings her talent for simple hilarity to the musical genre, dishing out the most delicious songs ever with titles such as "The Crabby Song," "Bad Babies," and "I Love You More Than Cheese." The tunes are singable, and the lyrics score eleven out of ten on the "funny-to-toddlers" meter.

Our family's favorite is "Tickle Time"; my boys loved it as toddlers, and we are still singing—and tickling—that tune ten years later. The lyrics are totally tickle-able ("Gitchy-gitchy goo . . .") with a tickle intermission to sign ("STOP, STOP, STOP"). Once you have mastered this ditty, you can sing a shortened version without the recording whenever you feel the need to tickle your toddler!

ALL-DONE

Dishes All Done by Lucia Monfried (Dutton Children's Books)
Yum, Yum, All Done by Jerry Smath (Grosset and Dunlap)

STOP

Bus Stops by Taro Gomi (Chronicle Books)
Next Stop by Sarah Ellis and Ruth Ohi (Fitzhenry and Whiteside Limited)
Red, Stop! Green, Go! by P. D. Eastman (Random House for Young Readers)
The Tale of Peter Rabbit by Beatrix Potter (F. Warne)

OUCH/HURT

Boo Hoo Boo-Boo by Marilyn Singer and Elivia Savadier (HarperFestival)
Bye-Bye, Boo Boo by David Prebenna (Golden Books)
Fundamental Toddler: Sam's Boo-Boo by DK Publishing (DK Children)
Ouch! by Ragnhild Scamell and Michael Terry (Good Books)

HOT

Bathwater's Hot by Shirley Hughes (William Morrow)

Hot, Cold, Shy, Bold: Looking at Opposites by Pamela Harris (Kids Can Press)

Hot Dog, Cool Cat: A Crazy Criss-Cross Book of Animal Opposites by Emma Dodd (Dutton Books)

One Hot Summer Day by Nina Crews (Greenwillow)

WHERE'S BABY?

WORDS TO LEARN: **EAT/FOOD, BOY, GIRL, APPLE/APPLESAUCE, BANANA, CEREAL, CHEESE, DRINK, MILK**
WORDS TO REVIEW: **SING/MUSIC, PLAY/TOY, MOMMY, DADDY, MORE, DOG, CAT, BALL**

You will need a cloth, scarf or small blanket for this chant.

One little baby boy [girl]	*Sign BOY [GIRL]*
Singing through the day.	*Sign MUSIC, tickling your child with the cloth*
Two little baby boys [girls]	*Sign BOY [GIRL]*
How they love to play!	*Sign PLAY, shaking the cloth*
Three little baby boys [girls]	*Sign BOY [GIRL]*
Eating with a spoon.	*Sign EAT, placing cloth to your lips (or child's)*
Four little baby boys [girls]	*Sign BOY [GIRL]*
Looking at the moon.	*Toss the cloth up in air and/or sign MOON**
My little baby boy [girl]	*Sign BOY [GIRL]*
Loves to hide from you.	*Place cloth over child's head*
Cover up my baby	
'Til Mommy [Daddy]	*Sign MOMMY [DADDY]*
says Boo!	*Pull cloth off quickly when saying "Boo!"*

Repeat using **GIRL** and **DADDY**.

*Add **MOON** sign to the performance of this tune after it has been presented (chapter 13).

By Anne Meeker Miller

EAT/FOOD

Place *gathered fingertips* to lips.

BOY

Close fingers to thumb at temple,
as if taking hold of the imaginary bill of
a ball cap.

GIRL

Drag thumb down side of cheek.

TIPS FOR INTRODUCING *WHERE'S BABY?*

○ Speak the chant very rhythmically. Try for a singsong vocal quality so that you are using the higher part of your vocal range.

○ I use tulle netting (very inexpensive material) in various colors for this song and game. I cut the cloth so that each piece is about four feet by four feet. The babies can then see their parent/caregiver through the transparent netting while they play "peek-a-boo." The tulle is also great for tactile stimulation.

○ If you have more than one cloth or scarf, give children a chance to pick the one they WANT—and sign WANT as you ask them which one they would like: "this one" (in my right hand) "or this one" (in my left hand)? This is also a great way to introduce colors ("You picked the blue scarf!")

○ Put the scarf, cloth or blanket across baby's legs. Set your child on your lap facing out.

○ Rock him side to side on your lap as you sign MUSIC for the singing line.

○ Give him a bounce or wiggle as you sign PLAY. You can also PLAY with the cloth in his lap by flapping or shaking it.

○ Gather the edge of the cloth in your hand, and bring it to your mouth or your child's mouth in a circular motion for "EATING with a spoon."

○ Throw the blanket into the air several times when you say, "Looking at the moon."

○ Place the cloth lightly over your child's head when you say, "My little baby loves to hide from you." Pull it off for "Boo!" Ask your child if he wants MORE. Then start from the top!

♪ More Musical Fun with *Where's Baby?*

ITEMS NEEDED: bed covers; set of five dogs, cats, or balls—can be pictures or small toys

- Let your child cover your head with the cloth and pull it off for "Boo."
- Make the chant into a bounce, adding more rhythmic experience for your child.
- Add this chant to your bedtime ritual using the bedcovers for the motions. The imagery is lovely, and you even have a moon to "look at" in the poem.
- Gather a set of five DOGs, CATs, or BALLs. They can be picture versions, but three-dimensional items are preferable. They do not need to be matching. Say the words to the "Where's Baby?" verse and change "baby" to the item you are holding, such as "Doggie," "Kitty Cat," or "bouncing ball." Hand one item to your child each time you count, and then perform its sign. Chances are your child will be watching you carefully to see if you will hand him another toy. This experience in one-to-one correspondence is an early math skill. It is also built-in repetition for practicing sign vocabulary!

LEARNING ABOUT MEALTIME: BABY BUFFET

Food signs are among the easiest to teach, because we are all interested and highly motivated learners when given the opportunity to get a tasty snack. Signs involved with mealtime—such as EAT, MORE, ALL-DONE, WANT, and PLEASE—are very motivating for babies to learn and will be among the first she will use in conversation with you. Babies love eating as much as adults do! Meals are also a great time for sign language learning,

because baby is contained in a high chair or booster seat and focused on you as you prepare her FOOD. Take advantage of your "captive audience" by signing to her as you get her meal ready and feed her. Here are some food signs good enough to EAT.

APPLE/APPLESAUCE

Twist knuckle of pointer on cheek.

BANANA

"Peel" pointer with *gathered fingers* of other hand.

CEREAL

Curve both hands with *fingers closed.*
Scoop one hand across the other and up
to mouth, as if eating cereal from a bowl.

CHEESE

Press palms of hands together
and twist, like pressing cheese.

DRINK

Bring *closed fingers* in "C" shape
to lips as if holding a cup.

MILK

Repeatedly squeeze one *closed
fist* as if milking a cow.

GAMES TO PLAY

♪ Peek-a-Boo Book

VOCABULARY PRACTICE: BOY, GIRL, DOG, CAT, FOOD

DEVELOPMENTAL BENEFITS: object permanence, problem solving, use of pictures to create meaning

MATERIALS: two-pocket plastic card protector sheet, pictures/drawings of chosen vocabulary words, felt or fabric squares, tape

DIRECTIONS: Draw or cut out a picture of words such as BOY, GIRL, or a FOOD item. Slip the pictures into the two pockets of the plastic page. Tape a square piece of felt or fabric along the top edge of each pocket so that it covers the picture. Ask your child to find the item you request by lifting the felt piece, or ask him to tell you the name of the object. Change the pictures periodically to maintain your child's interest in the peek-a-boo game.

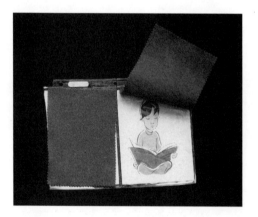

♪ Hide and Seek with Signs and Sounds

VOCABULARY PRACTICE: **TOY, CAT, DOG, BALL**
DEVELOPMENTAL BENEFITS: object permanence, focused listening skills
MATERIALS: colorful scarf or small blanket, small toy cat and dog, musical toy and ball

DIRECTIONS: Hide small toys or objects underneath a blanket or scarf. Ask the child: "Where's [TOY, CAT, DOG, BALL]?" The child can pull the blanket and search for the item you have requested. This is a great way to assess children's *receptive language,* or their ability to receive and understand the words you say to them. You can also have the child crawl or walk to the objects to extend the game.

Here is another way to play the game while enhancing your child's awareness of sounds. Hide a musical toy under the cloth and ask the child to "find MUSIC." The toy can be the wind-up variety, a small childproof instrument associated with MUSIC, or a homemade musical instrument. Repeat the game in different locations, and vary the places you hide the toy so that the game is challenging and fun.

"Hide and Seek" with objects is a
great game for teaching Ella to
understand words.

A SIGN OF SUCCESS

♪ CREATING TRADITIONS ♪

There's a place I can see in the best of my memory
Where it'll always be late in July.
When young love unconcerned with the ways of the world
was lost in a moment gone by.
So pardon me if I seem old-fashioned
In a world that's changing so fast.
Who would have ever imagined I'd be holding so tight to the past?

—"THE WAYS OF THE WORLD"

BY STEVE GILLETTE AND REX BENSON

Reading "The Night Before Christmas" is one of Kevin's favorite holiday traditions.

"Oh no, I've become my mother!" is a common—but seldom complimentary—refrain I hear from some of my female friends. In my case, it is my sincere hope that I do "become" my mother. She parented me perfectly. There isn't a thing about her I would have changed, and she is everything I hope to emulate in raising my own three children. Those of us who are fortunate enough to have been treasured by our parents as children can be transported back to a family memory in an instant—by a smell, a photo, hearing a familiar song, or returning to a place we once visited with our parents.

Most of us know instinctively what we should do to create family traditions. The process evolves as your family grows and you begin to develop lifelong friendships with your children. Your legacy will be the memories you create for them. Family rituals and special occasions are remembered and cherished in bits and parts—feelings, aromas, silly stories—as evidence of the constancy of the relationship your children have with you.

Becky Bailey, author of *I Love You Rituals,* reminds parents to focus on the purpose of family rituals: to connect with children through laughter, fun, relaxation, and sharing. Parents must be fully present with their children in these moments, clearing their minds of adult issues and responsibilities. Bailey also emphasizes the importance of coming to these experiences with no expectation other than great affection and acceptance of ourselves and our children at this moment in time where we deem everything that unfolds as "just right."

Sign language with young children is its own "love language." It is an experience that fosters the connection between family members and provides a means to share what is essential: "I care about you, little child, and I am here to help you figure out what you want and need." Sarah taught her firstborn daughter to sign despite the gentle protests her parents offered that doing so might delay her speech. When baby Tabitha surprised the entire family—as well as her pediatrician—by speaking early and often, her grandparents learned a few signs of their own and were ready when Tabitha's baby sister, Emma, was born two years later. Now signing is a fun and affectionate tradition for the entire family.

The beauty of *Baby Sing & Sign* is that the music and signing are equally important gifts for young families. There is a window of opportunity for using sign language with babies that lasts roughly twelve to eighteen months. However, the songs you sing with your child as you are engaged in the sign language learning process can last a lifetime. The music is a source of infinite fun and play as you add and change words to make them the unique musical property of your family.

When contemplating rituals and traditions for your young family, remember that the activity needs to be planned and repeated on a regular basis so that your child can look forward to its arrival. Every year my husband and I take our sons to a Christmas tree farm to select our tree. We must coordinate this outing in early December or—according to our sons—"there will be no trees left." Likewise, your child will begin to anticipate the special time you set aside to sing and sign with him. Melanie reported that her baby always began to smile and dance when she would put a CD in their player, because he was certain she would soon be making faces, laughing, playing games, and "doing lots of funny things with my hands" as she sang to him. There is nothing sweeter than anticipation.

> Family rituals and special occasions are remembered and cherished in bits and parts—feelings, aromas, silly stories—as evidence of the constancy of the relationship your children have with you.

And when it comes to life with young children—the simpler, the better. Life is complicated, and we need to model simplicity and serenity for our children. *Baby Sing & Sign* is meant to enhance your life by offering you a way to teach your child to communicate that is engaging and enjoyable. Take your time with the songs and the signs. Take a dance lesson from your child. Watch the way your child moves to her tunes with uninhibited exhilaration. Read and sign to her in the hammock on a cool morning in the backyard. Take her for a wagon ride after supper and count the DOGs and CATs you see in your neighborhood. Make your family pet a special cake for his birthday. Crawl with your child to the top of the stairs when it is time for BED (and always let her win.) Make sure you give your child at least seventeen hugs a day.

And remind yourself that in a few short years, your child will be passing the traditions you shared with her onto your grandchildren.

BOOKS TO READ

Children have their own special learning preference when it comes to exploring and figuring out their world: they like to look, listen, or do. Performing a task with their hands helps babies figure out how things work. Besides the pleasing taste of foods and the obvious need to satisfy a hungry appetite, young children love to eat because they can often feed themselves something yummy without assistance from others. And Cheerios are just the stuff to keep small fingers—and tummies—happy. *The Cheerios Animal Play Book* by Lee Wade (Little Simon) is a delicious little board book. There are crazy and colorful animals who need help from Baby to place Cheerios CEREAL in all the right places on each page. You don't need to tell Baby she is working on cool pre-math skills like pattern recognition and grouping, as well as practicing her fine motor skills. This is one book your child will ask (and sign for) by name: CEREAL!

EAT/FOOD

Gingerbread Baby by Jan Brett (Scholastic)

If You Give a Mouse a Cookie by Laura Joffe Numeroff (HarperCollins)

Sam's Cookie by Barbro Lindgren (HarperFestival)

Sesame Beginnings to Go: Time to Eat by Christopher Moroney (Random House Books)

Yummy Yucky by Leslie Patricelli (Candlewick Press)

BOY

A Boy and A Bear by Lori Lite (Specialty Press)

Be Boy Buzz by Bell Hooks and Chris Raschka (Jump at the Sun)

Gotta Have God: Fun Devotions for Boys Ages 2–5 by Lynn Ittner Klammer (Legacy Press)

The Biggest Boy by Kevin Henkes (HarperTrophy)

The Gingerbread Boy by Harriet Ziefert (Penguin Group)

The Puppy Who Wanted a Boy by Jane Thayer (HarperCollins)

GIRL

Daddy's Girl by Garrison Keillor (Hyperion)

Flower Girl by Laura Godwin (Hyperion)

Giddy Up, Cowgirl by Jarrett J. Krosoczka (Viking Juvenile)

Honey, I Love by Eloise Greenfield and Jan Spivey Gilchrist (Amistad)

I Want to Be a Cowgirl by Jeanne Willis and Tony Ross (Henry Holt)

Just Us Women by Jeannette Caines and Pat Cummings (HarperTrophy)

MISS MARY JANE

WORDS TO LEARN: CAR, WAGON, AIRPLANE

Riding in a buggy, Miss Mary Jane,
Miss Mary Jane, Miss Mary Jane,
Riding in a buggy, Miss Mary Jane,
We're a long way from home.

Verse 2. Riding in a car . . .
Verse 3. Riding in a wagon . . .

Gently bounce baby
Gently bounce baby
Gently bounce baby

Sign CAR throughout the verse
Sign WAGON throughout the verse

MISS MARY JANE

2. Riding in a car...
3. Riding in a wagon...
   Other ideas: truck, train, plane...

Traditional
Adapted by Anne Meeker Miller

CAR

Place *closed fists* in front of you and move them up and down alternately as if holding on to a steering wheel.

AIRPLANE

"Fly" *open hand* with ring and middle fingers folded down in an upward direction.

WAGON

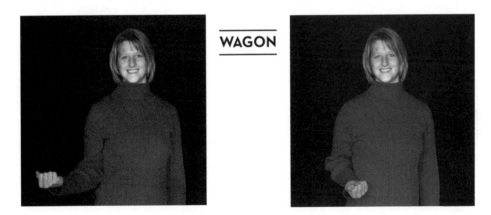

Move *closed fist* facing up toward body as if pulling a WAGON

TIPS FOR INTRODUCING *MISS MARY JANE*

○ Place your child on your lap facing out. Simply bounce him to the beat throughout the performance of the song. Perform signs with your hands in front of the child so he can watch and imitate your gestures. Sing and sign as you continue to bounce the child on your lap.

○ Toddlers will be able to maintain their balance on your lap while you bounce, sing and sign. They can steady themselves by putting their hands on your thighs or outstretched arms.

○ There is plenty of space in the lyric for your child's first and middle name ("Miss Anne Marie"). Change the rhythm of the song to best fit the cadence of your child's name.

♪ More Musical Fun with *Miss Mary Jane*

ITEMS NEEDED: large ball; toy dog or cat; wagon, bike, or stroller ("buggy"); laundry basket and towel or blanket

WAGONs are wonderful "baby buggies."

● Substitute anything you can think of for the "buggy" lyric, including nonsensical things such as clouds, camels, and carrots.

● You can also incorporate other baby signs and ride a DOG, CAT, or BALL. You may have "toy" versions of these items large enough to seat your child on so that the child can have a fun ride.

● "Miss Mary Jane" is the perfect music to travel by. Sing with gusto as you and baby take a trip to the park or through the neighborhood via WAGON, bike, or buggy. Be sure to synchronize the spring in your step to the beat of the tune. (Try to ignore passersby who stare in wonderment.)

● Laundry baskets make wonderful "buggies," CARs, WAGONs, AIRPLANEs, trucks, and trains. Place your toddler in a plastic laundry basket and add a folded towel or blanket underneath the "driver" for added stability. Give your child a push or pull around the living room. Make sure to add a sound so that your vehicle has an imaginary engine!

GAMES TO PLAY

♪ Rice Bin Dig

VOCABULARY PRACTICE: BOOK, BALL, TOY, CAR, AIRPLANE, WAGON

DEVELOPMENTAL BENEFITS: reach and grasp movements, tactile stimulation, object permanence, premath concepts

MATERIALS: plastic bin or other covered container; rice or dried oatmeal; small toys; books; items for scooping and pouring; plastic tablecloth/shower curtain

DIRECTIONS: Fill a large, covered container with rice or dried oatmeal. Gather small objects such as board BOOKs, BALLs, miniature TOY CARs, AIRPLANEs, WAG-ONs, or animals, butter bowls, and spoons and drop them into the bin.

Allow your child to experience the feel of the grain and practice the fine-motor skills of scooping and pouring. Place the bin on a large plastic tablecloth or shower curtain to make cleanup easier. Ask the child to find the item you request in the bin. You can also ask him to sign the name of the item he finds.

To ensure success, the requested item in the bin may be placed closest to the child. This is called "errorless learning." As the child is able to locate the requested item, the task can be made more challenging by moving the item farther away or hiding it under the rice.

A SIGN OF SUCCESS

♪ BOYS AND GIRLS MAY PLAY AND LEARN DIFFERENTLY ♪

What are little girls made of?
Sugar and spice and all things nice,
That's what little girls are made of.
What are little boys made of?
Snips and snails and puppy dog tails,
That's what little boys are made of.
—MOTHER GOOSE

The great debate among child development theorists has to do with "nature versus nurture," and whether our biology is more or less important than the opportunities in our environment that allow us to learn and grow. I remember very little from my first undergraduate course in psychology, but I do recall some discussion of *tabula rasa,* or blank slate. The belief forwarded by the philosopher John Locke (1632–1704) was that children begin life with no predisposition for intellect or behavior. Knowledge and character result from experience, thereby gradually filling the blank slate.

This notion fueled my premotherhood teaching, giving me reason to believe that all of my students had an equal opportunity to master the concepts and skills I taught. I still believe that all children can learn, but recognize that they benefit most from teaching methods that are customized to fit their unique learning styles and preferences. Some children learn best by listening to instructions, while others prefer to watch or actively participate in order to learn a new skill or concept.

The same holds true for parenting. The "handbook" you devise to guide your first offspring through childhood is suddenly obsolete when your second baby joins the family. The observations you make about your children the day they are born are often good predictions of the personality characteristics they will exhibit into adulthood. Remember the comments you and your family made to one another as you first checked out your new little one? After you made certain the baby had the requisite number of body parts while all marveled at his perfection, you might have used descriptors ranging from "mellow" to "active" or "eager." Are those traits still readily observable in your child today? The *tabula* your baby was issued at birth may not be as blank as Locke would have us believe.

It appears there are some enduring truths about raising girl- and boy-flavored babies as well. I am the mother of three sons, which proves that God has a sense of humor. I was raised with one female sibling, and was ill prepared for the rigors of being a mother of males. As a proud graduate of "The School of Motherhood," I have learned that boys and girls often learn in distinctly different—and gender-specific—ways.

Parents I've met who are vigilant about providing activities for their children that avoid gender stereotyping share similar stories. It does not seem to matter if you have carefully avoided all toys, games, and play activities that could be deemed "boy" or "girl." Your female child will still want to carry a purse. Your male child will want to point whatever he is holding in his hand at someone—often his grandmother—and make violent "pow pow" noises.

Studies investigating male and female biological differences, as well as the influence of experience and culture, usually raise more questions than they answer. While it is generally acknowledged that men and women use different parts of their brains to learn and problem-solve, it remains unclear to what extent environment and opportunity interact with biology in this process.

Michael Gurian, author of *The Wonder of Boys*, finds that boys are more spatial and visual in approaching games and thus require more physical space, whereas girls tend to be more verbal and emotional in their play. Boys often process their feelings through action, which translates to more observable gross-motor activity. Girls tend to be able to maintain interest in objects and fine-motor activity for longer intervals than boys, and are biologically inclined to be able to do several tasks at the same time. Gurian also suggests that girls generally are better at verbal tasks and reading, while boys tend to excel at spatial and analytical tasks such as math.

> As a proud graduate of "The School of Motherhood," I have learned that boys and girls often learn in distinctly different—and gender-specific—ways.

In his newest book, *Boys and Girls Learn Differently*, Gurian claims there are also gender differences in language development, with females producing more words than males. "We often find girls using words *as they learn*, and boys often working silently," he says.

Boys and girls may listen differently as well. Deborah, a primary-school teacher, reported that her male students seemed to listen better when they had something else to do at the same time, such as draw or take a walk.

If it is true that girls use more spoken words and show better fine-motor ability than boys, then they may biologically be at an advantage to sign sooner and more precisely. However, be careful not to jump to conclusions about your child based on research studies that cluster children into groups. Averages and estimates are of little help in inspiring the greatness within one baby boy or girl, as each child differs wildly from the next. The reality is that there are certain activities your child—whether boy or girl—will find inherently more interesting and engaging than others. Children must be engaged in an activity to learn. Learning is good. Ergo, roll with it.

Your boy child's favorite songs in this collection will probably be "Roll the Ball," "Miss Mary Jane," or any song involving motor skills such as running and jumping—so clear the "dance floor" and get ready to move! Your girl child may really like "Doggie, Doggie" or any song involving long, heartfelt conversations with her stuffed animals. Girls will also want to demonstrate their outstanding fine-motor skills, such as using sign language to communicate. And perhaps putting objects in and taking objects out of something . . . like a purse!

Miss Jaylie loves her fancy purse.

BOOKS TO READ

We judge how much we love books at our house by the condition of their binding. There are only a few fibers remaining on the binding of our *Cars and Trucks and Things That Go* by Richard Scarry (Random House Children's Books). Mr. Scarry is a genius at creating engaging and imaginative books for young readers. Each two-page spread of *Things That Go* contains hundreds of whimsical wheeled vehicles, including my favorite—the Pickle Car. There is also a small gold bug we called "Gold Buggie" to hunt for on each page.

Repetition is good. You will find wonderful song material for the "Miss Mary Jane" song in the pages of this book. Make the most of your child's developing love of books and music by singing new verses until it is your child's decision to stop the game. And be sure not to skip any pages!

CAR

Big Red Car by Bob Berry (Grosset and Dunlap)

Cars by Anne Rockwell (Puffin)

I Like Cars by Ladybird (Books Limited)

Miss Spider's New Car by David Kirk (Scholastic)

The Line-Up Book by Russo Marisabina (Greenwillow)

The Very Busy Life of Olaf and Venus: Car by Pierre Pratt (Candlewick Press)

WAGON

A Red Wagon Year by Kathi Appelt and Laura McGee Kvasnosky (Harcourt Childrens Books)

Farmer Palmer's Wagon Ride by William Steig (Farrar, Straus and Giroux)

My Little Wagon by Alma Powell and Marsha Winborn (HarperFestival)

Radio Flyer: My Red Wagon by Elizabeth Cody Kimmel and Rusty Fletcher (Dutton Juvenile)

Radio Flyer: My Wagon Will Take Me Anywhere by Elizabeth Cody Kimmel and Tom Newsom (Dutton Juvenile)

AIRPLANE

Angela's Airplane by Robert N. Munsch and Michael Martchenko (Annick Press)

Airplane Alphabet Book by Jerry Pallotta (Charlesbridge)

I Love Planes! by Philemon Sturges (HarperCollins)

Little Red Plane by Ken Wilson-Max (Cartwheel)

Planes by Anne Rockwell (Puffin)

THE LITTLE CAT GOES CREEPING

WORDS TO LEARN: **SLEEP/BED, FISH, THANK YOU**
WORD TO REVIEW: **CAT**

This is a traveling song, so hold your child or walk with him as you sing and sign.

The little cat goes creeping,	*Sign CAT as you tiptoe to the beat*
Creeping, creeping	*Continue to tiptoe*
The little cat goes creeping	*Sign CAT*
All through the house.	*Continue to tiptoe*

Verse 2. The little fish goes swimming
Verse 3. The little baby's sleeping

THE LITTLE CAT GOES CREEPING

The lit - tle cat goes creep - ing, creep - ing, creep - ing. The lit - tle cat goes creep - ing all through the house.

2. The little fish goes swimming...
3. The little baby's sleeping...
   (baby can also run, jump, march...)

Traditional
Adapted by Anne Meeker Miller

SLEEP/BED

Place *flat hand* palm-side up
on side of head and tilt head,
as if head rests on a pillow.

FISH

Hold one *flat hand,* thumb-side up,
with other *flat hand* touching at wrist.
Move both hands forward,
with front hand fluttering to imitate
fish swimming.

TIPS FOR INTRODUCING *THE LITTLE CAT GOES CREEPING:*

○ Carry your baby as you sing this song. Toddlers can do the walking themselves. Model the motions suggested by the song in an exaggerated fashion.

○ Let your movements mimic the music for each verse. For example, the CAT should creep on tiptoe at a moderate tempo. The FISH is a smoother gliding motion as he swims. The baby SLEEPING is a slower walk with an upper-body rock from side to side.

○ Finish the song by lying down on the floor for a nap. You can even lay your child on the couch or floor at the end. Cover the child with a blanket and tell her, "Night, night!"

○ Tell your child THANK YOU for PLAYing the CAT game with you. Ask her if she would like to PLAY some MORE.

○ Baby can also run, jump, march. Make up verses of your own!

♪ More Musical Fun with *The Little Cat Goes Creeping*

ITEMS NEEDED: basket, objects or pictures representing animal signs **(DOG, CAT, FISH)** and **GIRL** and **BOY**

● Make up verses for DOG, MOMMY, and DADDY. Ask your child to show you how she walks. Then think of an action word that matches her motion, and sing a new verse. For example, "The little DOG goes jumping."

● Make a "vocabulary basket" of animals. Put objects representing the signs you are teaching, such as Beanie animals or pictures, in a basket. Have your child take out DOG, CAT, and FISH and sing a verse for each. You can also include GIRL and BOY if you have dolls or pictures that can represent children.

● When you have played this game several times, ask your child to "find FISH" or ask, "Where is FISH?" This is a great activity for developing

Isaac will learn firsthand the meaning of the word FISH—how the fish looks, feels, and smells—as soon as he catches his first "whopper!"

receptive language learning (receiving and responding to a request) and listening skills.

- Select two objects and place them on the floor. The items may be positioned at a distance from your child, encouraging him to crawl or walk to the desired object. Ask him to "Get the FISH." A toddler may be able to sign or speak in response to the question, "Which one is FISH?"
- Sing the "Where's Baby?" song (chapter 7) and substitute FISH for BOY or GIRL.
- Add THANK YOU to communication with your child in response to any sign or vocalization he shares with you. This way, you are modeling the good manners you want your child to demonstrate with yourself and others.

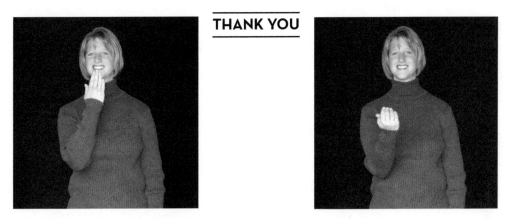

THANK YOU

Start *closed fingers* at mouth and move hand forward.

GAMES TO PLAY

♪ Baby Safari

VOCABULARY WORDS: DOG, CAT, FISH, PLAY, EAT, SLEEP/BED, MOMMY, DADDY

DEVELOPMENTAL BENEFITS: focused listening and looking, critical thinking, empathy for others

MATERIALS: map to the nearest petting zoo, stroller

DIRECTIONS: In the words of the immortal artists Marvin Gaye and Tammy Turell, "Ain't Nothin' Like the Real Thing, Baby." Take a field trip to your local petting zoo or farm so that baby can see firsthand how the animals move, what they EAT, and how they PLAY. Are the animals SLEEPing? Where is their BED? Which animal is a baby? Which animal is a MOMMY or a DADDY?

Listen carefully to how the animals sound as well. Try to imitate the sounds and see if your child will join in. Call his attention to the animals that make no sound at all. Focused listening and awareness of sound and silence are important fundamental music skills for young children.

You have mastered the animals in motion and met them "up close and personal." It is now time to play an animal sound game at home. Ask your child, "What sound does the CAT make?" Continue the game for all the animal signs you have learned. Play the game with other animals as well.

Trips to the petting zoo provide multisensory experiences for children—sounds, sights, smells, and more.

♪ Goldfish Bowls

VOCABULARY PRACTICE: **FISH, EAT, MOMMY, DADDY**

DEVELOPMENTAL BENEFITS: reach and grasp movements, eye-hand coordination, problem solving

MATERIALS: empty yogurt container, scissors, Goldfish or other snack cracker or cereal

DIRECTIONS: Place Goldfish or other snack crackers in an empty yogurt container. In attempting to get the snack, your child can practice reaching, pouring, and grasping. With the lid on, the container can be a shaker to accompany music. Toddlers will enjoy dropping the crackers or cereal into the container when a hole is cut in the lid.

Ask your child if he wants to EAT FISHies. Place the crackers on the high chair tray or table. Ask him to give a FISHie to MOMMY or DADDY. Give the child a few Cheerios along with the Goldfish crackers, and ask him to find the FISHie. Ask him what the FISHie is called.

A SIGN OF SUCCESS

♪ SIBLINGS CAN TEACH BABIES SIGN LANGUAGE, TOO! ♪

It is with our brothers and sisters that we learn to love, share, negotiate, start and end fights, hurt others, and save face. The basis of healthy (or unhealthy) connections in adulthood is cast during childhood.

—JANE MERSKY LEDER

Going from being the only child to the older sibling has its good days and bad. What a huge shock it can be to a youngster when his parents bring home a noisy blob in a blanket. No longer is former only child the center of the universe.

Amy recalls the day she and her husband brought their new infant son, Gianni, home from the hospital. Her nearly three-year-old daughter, Isabella (nicknamed Isa), looked more than a little alarmed. "When you bring your new baby home, the older kid looks at the baby like 'what is this?' and 'what do I do now?'" Amy said.

Gianni learns how to sign EAT from his older sister—and favorite sign language teacher.

Many older siblings will take on one of two roles when a new baby moves in: avid competitor or coparent. Sometimes it is the age difference that prompts the role, and sometimes it is the personalities of the children involved. Asking the sibling to help teach the new baby to sign is one way to encourage the coparent role. Now that Gianni is seven months old, Isabella enjoys reinforcing the signs that her mother is teaching by also using them in interaction with her brother.

Isa used sign language before she learned to talk but hadn't used the signs in more than a year. Amy was pleased to discover she only had to show Isa a sign one time before she would pick it right back up again. One day Isa saw Gianni advancing toward one of her books with a gleam in his eye. Rather than yelling or screaming at her baby brother, Isa made the sign for STOP. Her mother was pleased. "It's nice that she made the connection to use the sign instead of carrying on," Amy said. "Isa also signs MILK to Gianni, and he will kick his legs in anticipation, just as she did when she was a baby and I would sign MILK to her."

Darcy and David have three daughters, whom they taught to sign. According to Darcy, "The benefits are never-ending." Darcy has found that in making signing a family affair, there is never a breakdown in communication, and the baby's wants and needs can be met even if she is not standing right there. "For example," she said, "Mollie is in the high chair and I am cooking dinner. If she signs MILK and my other two girls see her, then they offer her the milk or they tell me." Darcy believes signing has helped her girls develop a very strong bond with one another by fostering playtime that's not always adult-driven but is instead extended from child to child.

> Signing helps children develop very strong bonds with one another while fostering playtime.

Kelly became interested in signing after the birth of her firstborn, Jack. She obtained books and taught herself and her son to sign. "I started with Jack when he was four months old. He's now three-and-a-half years old, and he has great verbal ability that I attribute to signing," she explained. Kelly recalls that Jack particularly used his signs when "he meant business." Now Jack is big brother to eighteen-month-old Ava, with all the duties and responsibilities that entails.

"I told Jack he had to help me sign with Ava because Mom was too busy sometimes," Kelly said. "He immediately picked up the signing again." Because Ava is Jack's little shadow, she is prone to emulate what she sees her brother doing—another benefit that siblings bring to *Baby Sing & Sign*. Ava participated in the *Baby Sing & Sign* class when she was six months old. Her mother said her signing peaked when she was ten to thirteen months old. Though she is now also honing her excellent verbal skills, Ava continues to sign, especially to her cousin, who is six months younger.

Siblings gain confidence when they share with and teach one another, and older children are natural role models for the young ones who follow. Parents can tap in to this natural tendency for the older child to lead, making the learning experience beneficial for all.

BOOKS TO READ

Hooray for wonderful books with big pages, colorful and fun illustrations, and verse that appeal to a toddler's sense of humor. And *Hooray for Fish* by Lucy Cousins (Candlewick Press). The author's FISH are "spotty" and "stripy," "happy" and "gripy"—and an entire school of other fun FISH described in rhyme. MOM and I LOVE YOU (chapter 13) are also included in the story. But please be warned: don't try to skip even one page of this book to hurry along your bedtime rituals. Your toddler will commit these lovely FISHies to memory quicker than your "baby FISH" can swim the length of your bathtub!

SLEEP

All on a Sleepy Night by Shutta Crum and Sylvie Daigneault (Stoddard)

Everyone's Sleepy by Ed Vere (Orchard Books)

I Am Not Sleepy and I Will Not Go to Bed by Lauren Child (Candlewick Press)

Snoozers by Sandra Boynton (Little Simon)

Ten in the Bed by David Ellwand (Handprint Books)

Time for Bed by Mem Fox (Harcourt Brace)

Time to Sleep by Denise Fleming (Henry Holt)

While You Were Sleeping by John Butler (Peachtree)

FISH

A Fish out of Water by Helen Palmer and P. D. Eastman (Random House Books for Young Readers)

Fish Eyes: A Book You Can Count On by Lois Ehlert (First Red Wagon Books)

Friendly Fish by Wendy McLean (Whitecap Books)

Ten Little Fish by Audrey and Bruce Wood (Blue Sky Press)

THANK YOU

Grateful: A Song of Giving Thanks by John Bucchino (HarperCollins)

Oops, Sorry! A First Book of Manners by Richard Morgan (Barron's Educational Series)

Richard Scarry's Please and Thank You Book by Richard Scarry (Random House for Young Readers)

Squirrel Says Thank You (First Virtues for Toddlers) by Mary Manz Simon, Linda Clearwater, and Kathy Couri (Standard Publishing)

Toby's Please and Thank You by Cyndy Szekeres (Little Simon)

10

BUNNY BOOGIE

WORD TO LEARN: **BUNNY**
WORD TO REVIEW: **EAT**

Hop like a bunny,	*Sign BUNNY*
Hop, hop, hop,	*"Hop" by bouncing baby or hopping*
Hop like a bunny,	*Sign BUNNY*
Hop, hop, hop,	*"Hop" by bouncing baby or hopping*
Hop like a bunny,	*Sign BUNNY*
Hop, hop, hop,	*"Hop" by bouncing baby or hopping*
Hop like a bunny,	*Sign BUNNY*
Hop, hop, hop,	*"Hop" by bouncing baby or hopping*
Verse 2. Wiggle your ears and hop . . .	*Sign BUNNY; then "Hop"*
Verse 3. Wiggle your tail and hop . . .	*Wiggle bottom; then "Hop"*
Verse 4: Chew your carrot [eat] and hop . . .	*Sign EAT; then "Hop"*
Verse 5: Hop like a bunny . . .	
Coda: I said you bunny,	*Sign BUNNY*
I love you, bunny,	*Sign I LOVE YOU and BUNNY*
You hippy, hoppy, funny bunny,	*Sign BUNNY*
Hop, hop, hop—Yeah!	*"Hop" then play "air guitar" on YEAH!*

BUNNY BOOGIE

Swing

D · · · · · · · · · · G · · · · · · · · · ·

Hop like a bun-ny, hop, hop, hop   Hop like a bun-ny, hop, hop, hop

D · · · · · · · A7 · · · G · D   2/4

Hop like a bun-ny, hop, hop, hop   Hop like a bun-ny, hop, hop, hop

2. Wiggle your ears and hop, hop, hop...
3. Wiggle your tail and hop, hop, hop...
4. Chew your carrot (eat) and hop, hop, hop...
5. Hop like a bunny, hop, hop, hop...

Coda Last Time

2/4 · · · E7 · · · · · · · A7 · · · · · ·

I said you   bun- ny__   I love you   bun- ny__   you

D   D7/F#   G   Gm   A7   D   DMaj7

hip- py, hop - py, fun- ny, bun- ny,   Hop,__ hop, hop   Yeah!

By Anne Meeker Miller

BUNNY

Closed fingers form bunny ears and wiggle backward at top of head.

Child may wiggle all five fingers with one or both hands, or place both hands by ears.

TIPS FOR INTRODUCING THE *BUNNY BOOGIE*

- ◯ Place baby on your lap facing out. Bounce her gently on the words "hop, hop, hop." Sign the word BUNNY as it occurs in the text.
- ◯ Babies who enjoy bearing weight on their feet can stand between your bent legs. Support the baby by placing your hands under her arms or on her rib cage. Bounce the baby gently, or hold her while she does the bouncing herself. Give the child an extra little lift on the words "hop, hop, hop."
- ◯ If you hold your child while doing the "Bunny Boogie," your hands will not be free to sign BUNNY. Use the sign at the end of the song in comments such as "Are you my BUNNY?" or "BUNNY hops!"
- ◯ Sign EAT for "Chew your carrot." You can make the gesture to your mouth or your child's mouth, as if you are feeding her the carrot.

♪ More Musical Fun with the *Bunny Boogie*

ITEMS NEEDED: food pictures cut from magazines or other sources, index cards, trading card plastic protector sheet

- Most toddlers enjoy trying to hop on their own while holding your hands. You can help the child hop by carefully holding her hand and lifting her on "hop, hop, hop."
- Extend the bunny fun while toning your thighs. Carefully but firmly hold your child in your arms, and hop with the child on "hop, hop, hop." Many children learn to hop independently with both feet together from around eighteen months to two years of age. This vicarious hop is a good simulation of their own future hopping and will show them that you know how to play!
- *I do not recommend children eating and hopping at the same time.* To use the "Bunny Boogie" to teach FOOD signs, cut pictures of your child's favorite food out of a magazine, mount them on index cards, and slip them into the pockets of a trading card plastic protector sheet. Ask your child to point to the food she wishes to sing about by signing *What do you WANT to EAT?* Once the child has made her selection, you can sing the song with her food choice: "Chew your CHEESE and hop, hop, hop!" This strategy makes food and hopping a safe, fun game. Your child is also exercising her musical "muscles" as she creates her own composition.

GAMES TO PLAY

♪ Baby's Play Book

VOCABULARY PRACTICE: MUSIC, MOMMY, DADDY, EAT

DEVELOPMENTAL BENEFITS: use of pictures to create meaning, prereading skills

MATERIALS: trading card plastic protector sheets used for musical instrument, family member, and food/hopping game; ribbon, plastic cord, or loose-leaf rings (and electrical tape)

DIRECTIONS: Several suggestions have been made throughout this book for using trading card plastic protector sheets:

"Clap Your Hands" musical instrument game (page 34)
"This Is the Mommy Wiggle" family member game (page 43)
"Hop Like a Bunny" food and hopping game (page 128)

Children enjoy a "play book" of their own. Here's how to make one. Take the pages from the games listed above, and fasten them together with ribbon, plastic cord, or loose-leaf rings. *If using the latter, be sure to tape the closed ends of the rings with electrical tape to prevent them from pinching or scratching your baby.*

One of the benefits of *expressive language,* or the ability to communicate our wants and desires, is the power to make choices. Children love to make decisions about the activities of their daily lives. The "play book" is a way for them to show you the game they want to play with you.

The book is also a wonderful prereading activity. It is never too early for children to learn that people and things they desire can be symbolically represented with pictures. The pictures will reinforce the sign language vocabulary you are teaching. Your child may require help manipulating the pages to make her game choice. Be sure to take the pages with you to the grocery store and allow your child to make food choices and add them to your shopping cart. Singing is allowed in most supermarkets.

Isa is in touch with her inner—and outer—BUNNY.

A SIGN OF SUCCESS

♪ FOSTERING YOUR CHILD'S CREATIVITY ♪

Imagination is more important than knowledge.
Knowledge is limited.
Imagination encircles the world.
—ALBERT EINSTEIN

My grandfather was a very funny guy. He took me to an amusement park when I was a pre-schooler and told me to wait in the car while he went for a pony ride. When I mentioned that I might like to take a pony ride as well, he pretended to be surprised that I would be interested in riding a pony, and then invited me to join him.

The following day, I called him to chat as I often did. During our conversation he said he was busy watching my grandmother ride a pony in their living room. I am told that I exclaimed, "Grandpa, I didn't know you had a pony!" And as you would expect, I imme-diately started pestering my mother to drive me at top speed to my grandparents' house. I wanted to see Grandma riding that pony for myself. I don't suppose my mother thought that Grandpa's game of pretend was as wonderful as I did that day.

Mine was a charmed upbringing filled with people who made it their mission to teach me the value of whimsy—the capacity for unrestrained imagination in the face of reason and reality. I had a rich variety of experiences and many opportunities to pursue activities that interested me. My ideas were valued and incorporated into our daily lives as a family. My artistic, musical, and literary creations were admired and shared with others in my circle of significant adults. Had baby sign language been "invented" and encouraged with babies of my generation, I am quite certain I would have signed with zest. I was a little girl with lots I wanted to do and say. I felt cherished and valued, and that is the safest of places to start from as you venture out into the world to try new things and explore the possibilities that life holds.

Humor, creativity, and imagination make a great difference in preparing children for a life of joy and adventure. They also have a powerful effect on the way we choose to play and communicate with the children we love. A baby's first smile—the kind you know was caused by amusement and not gas—is reason for celebration, and provides encouragement for parents and caregivers as they sense that their child notices them and finds them clever and interesting. Babies' smiles and giggles are truly addictive, prompting most of us to try out our entire repertoire of funny faces and fancy dances to get a reaction. Once we determine what makes our baby smile, we persist in doing it again and again. Similarly, the first time baby signs is a memorable occasion as well. Once you observe your child signing a single word, you will be hooked and want to teach her more words. When your child signs to you, it is proof of the powerful connection you two share and the realization that she is a clever being capable of inventing thoughts and ideas. No longer will you need to leave your home or turn on a television set for entertainment. All you need to do is put on the *Baby Sing & Sign* CD and hold hands with your spouse as you watch your child sing and sign with gusto in your living room.

> A parent or caregiver's ability to laugh and indulge in the unadulterated joy of life with children is a bonding experience like no other.

When babies smile, laugh, and sign with others, they are showing how much they take pleasure in social contact with people who care about them. But babies need to be taught how to "find the funny" in their daily lives. Researcher Carolyn Chaney explored how humor develops in infants and toddlers. She found that once babies can form expectations of what will happen next in their lives, they often laugh or smile when the unexpected occurs. When playing games such as "Hide and Seek" or "Chase," a child delights in the unexpected outcome—*How will my playmate find me?* The "baby humor" can be heightened when the playmate varies the outcome of the game by finding a new hiding place or altering how long the child must wait to be found. A verbal prompt such as "Are you teasing me?" or "You're a funny bunny" in response to your child's playfulness can also remind him of his own potential for humor and joking.

The many games described in this book provide ample opportunities for "humor education." Channel your inner clown as you engage your child in sign language learning by varying the ways you use your face, hands, and body to sign and play. Parents and caregivers can help children recognize humor by giving them cues. Exaggerated motions or facial expressions, as well as vocal inflection, help teach children to find the humor in a variety of experiences. Perhaps you and your child could take turns catching each other after a game of chase when you sing "Charlie Over the Water." The chase may last the entire song or end very quickly. The babies I know find this activity to be hilariously funny!

Developing your child's sense of humor will also help you keep yours, which comes in handy as you move through the more treacherous moments of parenthood. A parent or caregiver's ability to laugh and indulge in the unadulterated joy of life with children is a bonding experience like no other, and it's a wonderful attribute to share.

Laura Murphy, president of Real Families, Inc., shares a great story about the importance of humor in her family. "From the time our kids were babies, they have sensed and participated in the warmth of humor in our household. However, I've never heard it more eloquently put as it was described by our ten-year-old son. One night, after a particularly fun dinnertime at our house, my son said to me, 'Do you know what I love best about Dad? It's that he can make us laugh so hard that I feel as if I don't know where my next breath is going to come from. It really is the greatest feeling in the world.'"

Once a child learns to play his own "jokes" with pretending games—learning that his rubber duckie can quack, that he can make his stuffed animal hop like a BUNNY, and that Daddy will never find a boy who hides in a laundry basket—parents and caregivers can begin to nurture this creativity in other ways as well. Karen Miller, a child development specialist, suggests that parents encourage children's creativity and imagination by helping them:

○ Feel valued
○ Explore space and direction through motor movement
○ Have opportunities to hold and manipulate objects and materials
○ Make a mess
○ Enjoy a variety of experiences

In his book *Playful Parenting*, Lawrence Cohen describes play as "a place of magic and imagination where a child can be fully one's self." A youngster who impersonates a monkey or who sings from the top of the "mountain" as she plays on the swing set in her backyard is honing her skills for innovation and originality. Parents who join in these games can relive play memories from their own childhood and have a lot of fun in the process. It is no coincidence that play is one of the core experiences of *Baby Sing & Sign*. Imaginative play allows a child to "test drive" his ideas without fear of the judgments and boundaries we associate with the real world. Sign language can be another tool for children to use in order to share their imagination and creativity as they use their words as "building blocks" to problem-solve, reason, and dream.

Music can provide wonderful opportunities for imagination and creativity. Marjorie, a veteran teacher in music as well as preschool and elementary teaching, believes rhythm comes first as young children begin to create music. For example, they can pat a playful beat as they sing or tap a tune all their own using their spoon and high chair tray. Sound play and creation of movements to accompany singing are also favorite activities of very young children. She often asks her youngest students to make up songs using their "show and tell" items for musical inspiration. She writes down the songs for them to keep and share with their families.

Get in touch with your inner toddler. Revisit that creative, enthusiastic youngster you were many years ago, and invite her to make a play date with the baby at your house. Children whose families foster their creativity and imagination incorporate those competencies into their sense of self.

Marjorie shared a humorous story about one of her three-year-old students who was hard at work creating an art project with markers, glue, and buttons. Marjorie commented, "You are doing such a nice job on your picture."

The little girl replied: "Thank you. I've been an artist all my life."

Laughter is music to the ears of a young child!

BOOKS TO READ

My favorite books are those that take me to places I can only visit in my imagination. The adventure of riding the dusty trail on my horse is only a dream for this city girl. But thanks to *Cowboy Bunnies* by Christine Loomis (Puffin Books), your baby broncobuster will experience all the thrills of "home on the range." The lively verse reads like a square dance call as the "cow-BUNNY" rides his pony, does his chores, cooks his lunch over a campfire, and takes a nap in the shade. I read this book to toddlers with my best Texas accent, although some would argue that my own Kansas accent is plenty credible for this here BUNNY ballad.

BUNNY

Bunnies on the Go by Rick Walton (HarperCollins)

Bunny Mail by Rosemary Wells (Viking Penguin)

Bunny My Honey by Anita Jeram (Candlewick Press)

Bunny's Noisy Book by Margaret Wise Brown (Hyperion Books for Children)

If You Were My Bunny by Kate McMullan (Scholastic)

Pat the Bunny by Edith Kunhardt Davies (Golden Book)

So Many Bunnies by Rick Walton (HarperFestival)

The Runaway Bunny by Margaret Wise Brown (Harper and Row)

11

CHARLIE OVER THE WATER

Charlie* over the water,
Charlie over the sea,
Charlie catch a fishie,
Can't catch me!

Sign WATER
Sign WATER
Sign FISH
Shake head side to side as if saying
"No way!"

*Substitute your child's name, **MOMMY**, **DADDY**, **DOG**gie, or **CAT** (kitty).

CHARLIE OVER THE WATER

Char - lie ov - er the wa - ter,

Char - lie ov - er the

sea,_____ Char- lie catch a fish - ie,

Can't catch me!

Substitute your child's name, mommy or daddy

Traditional
Adapted by Anne Meeker Miller

WATER

Tap pointer of *open fingers* on the middle of your chin several times.

Child may tap chin with all four fingers or *gathered fingertips.*

TIPS FOR INTRODUCING
CHARLIE OVER THE WATER

○ This song should be sung with the proper enthusiasm due a wonderful old sea chantey. Sing the lyrics with an accented quality, as if you are rowing a boat to the beat of the tune.

○ Change "Charlie" to your child's name. You can also substitute MOMMY and DADDY.

○ Sign WATER as it occurs in the song.

○ This can also be a fun "baby bounce." Give your child a bounce each time you sing the word "Charlie."

♪ More Musical Fun with *Charlie Over the Water*

ITEMS NEEDED: bathtub or swimming pool, water toys, blanket (preferably blue)

- Try playing a marching "Follow the Leader" game as you sing. Make your march go high and low by standing on your tiptoes and bending your knees. You can even add a jump on your child's name.
- Try another game called "Catch Charlie." Sing the song through, and when you get to "can't catch me," start running and see if your child will follow. When the child "catches" you, he gets to be the leader and run next.
- Sing your Charlie song in the WATER during bath time or a trip to the swimming pool. Add toys and mix thoroughly with PLAY!
- Your toddler will enjoy a crawling game that teaches *over, under,* and *around* as well. Sing "Charlie Over the WATER" and help your child climb *over* the top of a blanket. (A blue blanket would be great to represent the blue WATER of the ocean if you have one handy.) Play the game again, but ask your child to climb *under* the blanket, or crawl *around* the blanket.

GAMES TO PLAY

♪ Rub-a-Dub-Dub . . . Sign Language in a Tub

VOCABULARY PRACTICE: FISH, WATER, CAR, DOG, CAT

DEVELOPMENTAL BENEFITS: ability to manipulate objects, sensory experience

MATERIALS: plastic cars, animals, and balls; shallow plastic bins; sponges; pouring containers

DIRECTIONS: In a shallow plastic bin filled with one or two inches of water, place plastic toys or other objects corresponding to signs the child is learning . Cookie cutters make good toys for this game, as do small plastic cars, animals, and balls. Be sure to include some objects that float and others that do not. Sponges to squeeze and containers for pouring and filling are great to encourage fine-motor activity.

Sing the lyric, "Charlie catch a FISHie, can't catch me!" See if your child will find the FISH in the WATER and hand it to you. You can substitute other sign vocabulary for FISHie, such as race CAR or DOGgie.

As with all the activities described in this book,
take great care in supervising young children during water play.

♪ Water Bottle Toy

VOCABULARY PRACTICE: WATER, TOY, FISH

DEVELOPMENTAL BENEFITS: awareness of cause and effect, focused looking, sensory enjoyment

MATERIALS: clear plastic bottle, water, light corn syrup or vegetable oil, food coloring, sequins or other small objects such as plastic fish, glue gun

DIRECTIONS: Fill a clear plastic bottle with water and light corn syrup. Add food coloring and glitter as desired. Place small plastic fish in the bottle so that your child can watch them "swim." (Vegetable oil and water may be combined for the same effect.) Firmly attach the water bottle top using a glue gun.

Ask your child if she wants to play with her WATER or FISH TOY. Tell her to watch the FISHie swim in the WATER. See if she will point to the FISHie in the bottle when asked.

A SIGN OF SUCCESS

♪ GRANDPARENTS GET INVOLVED ♪

I'll love you dear, I'll love you
Till China and Africa meet,
And the river jumps over the mountain
And the salmon sing in the street.
—"AS I WALKED OUT ONE EVENING," W. H. AUDEN

There's something extra special about a grandparent's love—in its constancy and the unconditional way that it's bestowed. Looking back, I know my two grandmothers were one of the greatest blessings of my childhood. My grandmothers made me feel special, made me feel significant, made me feel *heard*. I could talk to my grandmothers about things I would never bring up to my parents. My grandmothers were far less critical.

That is the role of a grandparent. Parents have the responsibility, grandparents have the fun . . . as well as the perspective that comes from having raised children to adulthood and knowing in retrospect what is truly important. In today's society, more mothers work outside the home and more grandmothers are stepping into the role of caregiver. Sign language can help bridge the communication as well as the generation gap for these grandparents. While parents typically initiate the *Baby Sing & Sign* program at home, grandparents, too, can have fun reinforcing sign language learning with baby.

Grandparents get "on board" with *Baby Sing & Sign*

Susan keeps her grandson, Quinten, three days a week. She heard about the *Baby Sing & Sign* classes and thought taking the class and teaching the signs would help Quinten develop his language skills. "I thought the class was wonderful," Susan said. "I loved the way it was set up and especially enjoyed watching Quinten mixing with the other kids." Quinten and his grandma now listen to the *Baby Sing & Sign* CD every day. Quinten loves the songs and will start clapping as soon as the music begins. Grandma loves how the songs help her remember the signs. "When I turn on the music, I remember the signs," she said.

Karen is her granddaughter's full-time caregiver. She and Allison took the *Baby Sing & Sign* class when Allison was eleven months old. "It was fun getting her out," Karen said. "Grandmas can give more attention than parents sometimes can." Allison likes watching her grandma do the signs during the songs. She points to the CD player when she wants to hear the songs. "She definitely enjoys the music," her grandmother noted. "She'll sit and move. She watches me when it's time for the sign—she anticipates what is coming." Now almost a year old, Allison can sign PLAY and MORE, the latter especially when she is eating. "Using MORE was a big deal," Karen recalled.

Grandparents can have fun reinforcing sign language learning with baby.

Ann occasionally cares for two grandbabies: Lauren is fifteen months old, and her cousin Sophia is five weeks younger. The girls took the *Baby Sing & Sign* classes with their mothers, but Ann knew she needed to know the signs, too. Ann believes the signing has been very helpful—alleviating a lot of frustration for her grandchildren. Signing also makes mealtime a cleaner experience at Ann's house. She now waits for Lauren to sign MORE before giving her a second helping of food. When Lauren is finished eating, she signs ALL-DONE and Grandma Ann clears the tray. Before learning to sign, Lauren's method of announcing that the meal was over was to throw the leftover food on the floor. Ann's grandchildren also now ask to go outside by touching the door and signing PLEASE, a sweet gesture Ann finds difficult to resist.

One day Lauren attended a sporting event with her parents and grandparents in another town. A little bored, the toddler began walking around, eventually joining another family that was seated on a blanket nearby. The father, after asking Lauren's mother for permission, offered Lauren a snack. Ann watched as Lauren ate the snack, then approached the man and signed MORE. She continued making the sign while getting closer and closer to him. "She was talking to him with her sign," Ann said. "And I thought, this little girl knows how to get what she wants within the framework of language she knows."

To babies, grandmas and grandpas have always been capable of doing wondrous things. Now, with programs like *Baby Sing & Sign* grandparents and their grandbabies can learn to do wondrous things together.

BOOKS TO READ

"There's a little white duck sitting in the WATER, a little white duck doing what he ough-ter. . . ." Walt Whippo and Bernard Zaritzky wrote this classic children's song in 1950, and we've been singing it ever since. If you can't quite remember this melody, you can listen to the tune online at the National Institute of Environmental Health Sciences Kids' Pages (www.niehs.nih.gov/kids/lyrics/littlewhite.htm), along with hundreds of other folk songs for children.

Joan Paley fluffs this old duck's feathers and adds a guitar-playing mouse to narrate her rendition of *The Little White Duck* (Little, Brown). I give this book an enthusiastic "thumbs up" for creating opportunities for children to play with the sounds the animals make, but I must give it a "PG" rating because one critter does EAT another. However, they all return for their curtain call on the final page—including the one who meets his demise earlier.

You simply must *sing* this story to your baby—no boring speaking voice allowed. Paley includes a musical score for those who read music, but baby only expects your enthusiastic best effort. If a guitar-playing mouse can sing this story, so can you!

WATER

A Fish out of Water by Helen Palmer and P. D. Eastman (Random House Books for Young Readers)

Maisy Goes Swimming by Lucy Cousins (Little, Brown)

No More Water in the Tub by Tedd Arnold (Puffin Books)

Rub a Dub Dub by Kin Eagle (Whispering Coyote Press)

The Water Hole by Graeme Base (Puffin Books)

Water Play by Margaret Miller (Little Simon)

Water, Water by Eloise Greenfield and Jan Spivey Gilchrist (HarperFestival)

12

MY WORLD

WORD TO LEARN: **BOOK**
WORDS TO REVIEW: **SONG, BALL, PLAY, BOY, GIRL, BED/SLEEP**

My world, my world,
Songs for singing in my world.
My world, my world,
Songs for singing in my world.

Verse 2. . . . Balls for playing . . .
Verse 3. . . . Boys and girls . . .
Verse 4. . . . Beds for sleeping . . .
Verse 5. . . . Books for reading . . .
Verse 6. . . . Hmmm [music] . . .

Sway side to side
Sign MUSIC
Sway side to side
Sign MUSIC

Sign BALL and PLAY
Sign BOY and GIRL
Sign BED/SLEEP
Sign BOOK
Sign MUSIC

MY WORLD

2. Songs for singing
3. Balls for playing
4. Boys and girls
5. Beds for sleeping
6. Hmmm (music)...

By Anne Meeker Miller

BOOK

Place palms together and then open them as if opening up a book.

Child may either place palms open or closed, but not do the opening motion.

TIPS FOR INTRODUCING *MY WORLD*

○ Hold the child on your lap and rock side to side as you sing. Demonstrate the signs for your child by holding your hands in front of her body so that she can see and touch them.

○ Help your child form the signs by gently guiding both of her little hands with yours.

○ "My World" is a great song for practicing sign language with baby. As you master new signs, you can add verses. Let this be the "theme song" of your signing experience.

○ Sign MUSIC on the improvised humming verse of the song.

♪ More Musical Fun with *My World*

ITEMS NEEDED: poster board or card stock paper, pictures representing things or activities from child's life, bulletin board for child's room

- Alter the tempo or quality of the song to keep it musically interesting. For example, try making your singing smoother or more accented as if marching. You could even make the song into a "baby bounce" by adding an up-and-down motion with your knees. Make an even smoother version by exaggerating your swaying from side to side.

- Take a walk around your baby's "world" outdoors. Ask your child to point to things he sees as you travel, and make up a new verse for each, such as "grass for growing . . ." or "DOGs for petting in my world."

- Make a small poster of pictures that represent important objects or people in your child's life, such as MOMMY, DADDY, DOG, or BOOK. Put the poster in a plastic page cover to make it last longer. The pictures on the poster do not need to represent sign language vocabulary, but can be another opportunity for practice. Ask the child to point to a picture on the poster, and then sing a "My World" verse about it.

- You can also make a bulletin board over the changing table consisting of interesting pictures from baby's "world." Change them periodically to maintain his interest.

Mom makes reading an essential component of Anthony's daily routine.

GAMES TO PLAY

♪ My World Waits

VOCABULARY PRACTICE: SONG, BALL, PLAY, BOY, GIRL, BED/SLEEP

DEVELOPMENTAL BENEFITS: focused listening, anticipation of predictable musical events

MATERIALS NEEDED: none

DIRECTIONS: Here is a fun game to play while waiting at a doctor's office, the auto repair shop, or some other location not optimally suited for young children to roam. This activity requires no props or preparation. Position the baby on your lap facing out. Once you and baby have learned the "My World" song, hum the melody softly in your baby's ear as if you are telling her a secret. Rock the child gently from side to side as you quietly sing.

When you get to the place in the song where you would sing the words you are learning in sign, place your hands in front of your child and perform the sign. Sing the verses in the sequence you have practiced at home. Depending on the child's age and opportunities to practice, she may anticipate the sign that comes next. That is, she may sign the word that comes next or shape your hands into the sign, indicating that she is able to practice a song internally without support from the lyrics. In its purest form, a child practices the song in her mind without hearing a note. This "singing in your head" activity is great for developing sequencing skills, sign vocabulary, and musical memory.

Grandmother Karen sings quietly
to Allison while they wait at the doctor's office.

♪ Homemade Playdough

VOCABULARY PRACTICE: PLAY, ALL-DONE, DOG, CAT, BALL, FISH
DEVELOPMENTAL BENEFITS: tactile stimulation, creativity
MATERIALS/INGREDIENTS:

1 cup flour
1 cup warm water
2 teaspoons cream of tartar
1 teaspoon oil
1/4 cup salt
food coloring
flavoring, spices, or powdered drink mix (optional)

DIRECTIONS: Mix all ingredients together, adding food coloring last. Stir over medium heat until smooth and forming a ball in the pan. As soon as it is cool enough to handle, remove dough from pan and knead. Place in plastic bag or airtight container when cooled. The dough will last for a long time, and is perfectly safe for baby to taste.
VARIATIONS: Put in two packages of powdered drink mix to add smell as well as color. Include food coloring and spices to provide more sensory interest for your child. Try cinnamon, pumpkin pie spice, or extracts such as peppermint, lemon, orange, or strawberry.

The coolness and texture of the playdough provides "finger fun" for Isaac.

Ask your child if she would like to PLAY with PLAY dough. Allow your child to push the dough with her fingertips or hold a small ball of the mixture in her hand. She can also use her palm to flatten the dough ball on the surface of her high chair or your kitchen counter or table top. You can also help her roll the dough and use cookie cutters in the shape of DOG, CAT, BALL, or FISH. Watch for her to tell you she is ALL-DONE with her dough play.

Many children are hesitant initially to play with dough. The texture may be overwhelming to their sensitive fingertips. Others may enjoy dough play but be overwhelmed if you add scents or colors to the mixtures with spices and drink mixes. Be sure to go slowly with dough play and to be observant of your child's reactions. Also consider that spices and drink mixes could stain clothing or table and counter tops. Perhaps dress your child in a "sloppy shirt" for dough play!

A SIGN OF SUCCESS

♪ BUILDING UNDERSTANDING BETWEEN DEAF ♪ AND HEARING CHILDREN

One-year-old Ava and her family were enjoying a dinner at their favorite restaurant. Ava's parents were "chatting" with her using the baby signs she had enthusiastically mastered. Also enjoying a meal out that evening was a group of older deaf adults. They approached the family to ask whether Ava was deaf and began to engage them in a conversation using sign language, lip reading, and pantomime.

Ava's mother was able to sign "baby," and the deaf adults taught her the sign for the word "sign." Ava and her family shared their entire repertoire of sign vocabulary, including all the animals they had learned, to the amusement and amazement of the deaf adults, who in turn taught the family some new signs. Ava's parents sensed that the deaf adults were thrilled and grateful that sign language was an essential part of the daily lives of a hearing family. One member of the group assured Ava's mother that signing would "increase the baby's intelligence." It was a wonderful experience for all.

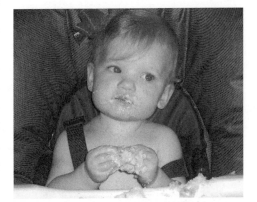

Ava shared her baby sign—MORE
—with her new deaf friends.

The benefits of using signs based on American Sign Language with babies are numerous. This form of signed communication uses hand shapes that are simple to use and more compatible with baby's developing fine-motor skills. The prevalence of ASL in the United States, and its popularity as a language with hearing as well as deaf children, makes the gestures easily recognizable as children move from home to daycare, or change from one daycare setting to another.

Darcy is a deaf educator who works primarily with deaf toddlers. She taught her three hearing daughters baby sign language and teaches classes and workshops on sign language to hearing children. She has used the *Baby Sing & Sign* program extensively with her students who have received cochlear implants, and reports that it has been helpful in teaching them how to listen. For example, "This Is the Mommy Wiggle" helps students recognize the difference in the vocal qualities of a man, woman, and child. "The Little Cat Goes Creeping" helps them hear changing tempos or speed fluctuations in the music. In addition, Darcy believes the program's emphasis on focused listening has been invaluable to her students and finds that hearing children experience the same benefits. Just as for hearing children, a combination of speech and sign is used to realize the goal of spoken communication.

Robin is an interpreter and preschool teacher at a state school for deaf students. She is also the mother of a deaf child. She believes that ASL sets the tone for language development and allows both hearing and deaf children to acquire communication skills in a natural way. The hand shapes are "unmarked," which means they require no knowledge of the signed alphabet. They give children communication facility that is precise, immediate, and easily recognized by family members and caregivers, as well as those in the deaf community.

> The prevalence of ASL in the United States, and its popularity as a language for hearing as well as deaf children, makes the gestures easily recognizable.

Robin and Darcy agree that baby signing has been greeted enthusiastically by the deaf community. The hope is that teaching young hearing children to sign will help to break down stereotypes and barriers. Unfortunately, social communication between hearing and deaf children in school settings can sometimes be a negative experience. The deaf child feels like an outsider, and the hearing child is uncertain or fearful of what is expected of him. Therefore, teaching hearing children to sign to their deaf peers can help all children feel included and their contributions valued. Sign language provides the visual experience necessary for both hearing and deaf children to participate enthusiastically in my preschool music classes. The form and predictability of music make it easy for children to remember what comes next as they all enthusiastically sing with both their hands and their voices.

Many secondary and some elementary schools are starting to include ASL instruction in their curriculum. With the move toward inclusion of all children in the general education classroom, regardless of their disability, there is an increased likelihood that hearing and deaf children will have the opportunity to interact and learn together. Giving hearing children the tools to communicate with their deaf peers will provide a bridge of understanding that will lead to shared experience and mutual respect. And that spells friendship in any language.

BOOKS TO READ

Most parents of young children are familiar with Margaret Wise Brown's wonderful picture book *Goodnight Moon*. Brown wrote another book called *My World* (HarperFestival, 1949) that shares the same style of prose and illustration. Both you and your child will enjoy reading *My World*. Its text includes much of the sign vocabulary selected for the *Baby Sing & Sign* program, providing an interesting way to practice sign language.

BOOK

Being Me by Julie Broski (Scholastic)

But Excuse Me That Is My Book by Lauren Child (Tiger Aspect Productions)

Bunny's Noisy Book by Margaret Wise Brown (Hyperion)

I Like Books by Anthony Browne (Candlewick Press)

My Book Box by Will Hillenbrand (Harcourt Brace)

The Best Place to Read by Debbie Bertram and Susan Bloom (Random House)

13

SKYE BOAT LULLABY

WORDS TO LEARN: **STARS, BLANKET, MOON, I LOVE YOU**
WORDS TO REVIEW: **MUSIC, WATER**

Speed, bonnie boat, like
   a bird on the wing.
"Onward," the sailors cry.
Carry the babe that's born to be king
   over the sea to Skye.
Bright the STARS shine.   *Sign STARS*
Lightly we sail.
Quiet the waves roll by.
BLANKET for baby,   *Sign BLANKET*
Hug and a kiss [I LOVE YOU]   *Sign I LOVE YOU*
MOON sings a lullaby [MUSIC]   *Sign MOON and MUSIC*

SKYE BOAT LULLABY

Traditional
Adapted by Anne Meeker Miller

Move both lifted pointers up and down
"in the sky."

STARS

Child may lift one hand or both and
wiggle fingers over head.

TIPS FOR INTRODUCING *SKYE BOAT LULLABY*

○ This is a "listening song" for you to share at a tender time in your day, such as before naptime, bedtime, or some other snuggle occasion. I have shared signs to perform as you sing, but truly think it is best to just sit in a rocking chair and hum or sing along softly as you rock. Many families use the CD performance of this song as a part of their nighttime rituals.

○ Dim the lights and snuggle into a rocking chair. Rock rhythmically and gently in time with the tune.

○ If you like, gently add the signs for STARS, BLANKET, MOON, I LOVE YOU and MUSIC ("lullaby") as you sing the lyrics or hum the tune.

○ Hum or sing quietly in your child's ear.

○ The violin playing is beautiful and very soothing. When the violin plays its special solo section, you can sign MUSIC for baby to see.

○ Always conclude the song with an I LOVE YOU hug. However, the sweetness of this intimate musical moment between you and your child will communicate your feelings more expressively than your spoken words.

♪ More Musical Fun with *Skye Boat Lullaby*

○ This lovely old ballad tells the story of Bonnie Prince Charlie, who escaped from the Scottish mainland to the Island of Skye after he was defeated in battle.

○ Set aside any misguided belief you hold that you are not a good enough singer to sing to your children. They believe you are the best singer in the world. They associate you with smiles, kisses, good smells, and beautiful music. There is no voice they prefer to yours.

○ Provide a prelude to this bedtime lullaby by singing the song during bath time. Add a boat to your bath toys and let your child be the boat's captain! This practice provides a lovely and natural transition from bath to bedtime rituals.

 **BLANKET**

Two hands pretend to pull a blanket up from chest to beneath chin.

LEARNING ABOUT BEDTIME

The structure and predictability of music is comforting to your child, as is the sight and scent of you. From the perspective of babies, there is very little in their world that they can control. The events of their lives seem to be a constant bombardment of random activity. That is why your nighttime routine is such a cherished part of their day. They can expect that after a bath and nighttime nursing, bottle or snack come books and holding. Be consistent with your nighttime rituals. Do not skip any steps, and most certainly do not forget to sing!

Lullabies are the ultimate expressive experience. Parents are able to communicate deep affection for their child in a way that only music makes possible. The benefits of singing lullabies to your child have more to do with strengthening the bond between the two of you and providing comfort than with developing music or language skills.

Your nighttime ritual should include a repertoire of lullabies that will be a precious part of baby's earliest childhood memories. Remember that you are your child's first and best music teacher. The lullabies you sing with your child will be the same ones he will sing to his own babies.

Your child enjoys the sensation of your singing. With his back to your chest, he can feel you breathe and experience the resonance of your singing against his skin. This will remind him of a time not long ago when you rocked him as he floated in the womb, and when the distant sound of your voice was the only music he knew. The rhythm of your singing was the beat of your heart. Rock on.

WATER was the first sign "Bonnie Prince" Andrew's parents observed him use in signed communication with them.

GAMES TO PLAY

♪ Moon Walk with Baby

My firstborn son received most of the toys available commercially during his first two years of life. Such is the fate of a first grandchild! Among all of these riches, one of his favorite "toys" was the actual, honest-to-goodness MOON (the one you see in the sky on a cloud-less night). My husband made a game of searching our backyard with Andy, looking for the moon. On cloudy nights, when the MOON was nowhere to be found, he would tell our son that the bad guys had stolen it. (My husband watches too many James Bond movies.)

There is something magical about the MOON. Hum or sing "Skye Boat Lullaby" to your child outside under the moonlight on a mild evening.

MOON

Form a "C" with pointer and thumb, and lift this "crescent moon" over head.

Child may simply lift hand over head.

I LOVE YOU

Both *closed fists* cross chest, as if hugging self.

Child may pat upper chest with palms.

A SIGN OF SUCCESS

♪ LEARNING AT A NATURAL PACE ♪

Our children are like butterflies—quite beautiful in their own ways, in their own time. They should not be pushed to preen, or to fly, before they are ready.
—ALVIN ROSENFELD AND NICOLE WISE

Often the unique soul of a child gets lost amid all the pushing and directing and orchestration of his or her upbringing. Children want nothing more than to please their parents and will go to great lengths to try not to let them down, even if it is holding them back from what they'd rather be doing.

"There is great value in quiet moments."

There's a saying I've always loved—something about how parents don't own their children, God just loans them for eighteen years. Part of the delight in being in the company of kids is the opportunity to see them as the unique individuals they are: what gifts they were born with, what lessons they are here to teach us, and what lessons we can help them learn. For that reason, I believe the best role parents can play is that of guide. By introducing them to the world, answering their questions, accepting them with an open heart, and exposing them to a wide range of experiences, parents allow children freedom to find their own opportunities to blossom and grow.

As child psychologist William Crain, PhD, points out in his book *Reclaiming Childhood,* with each passing year our society is placing greater importance on preparing children for their life as adults instead of just embracing and enjoying them during this youthful and creative time in their lives. Writes Dr. Crain, "In today's world, children's present interests and feelings count for little in comparison to the all-important goal of preparing them for the adult workplace." Crain goes on, "We are so preoccupied with their future that we cannot see and value them for who they are, children."

Cindy Giddings has a master's degree in special education and is cocreator of the *Baby Sing & Sign* program. As the mother of a young son, she is increasingly troubled by what she sees as a generation of children who are grossly overscheduled. "I'm beginning to see parenting skill measured by how many activities parents schedule for their kids," she commented. "One does not accurately reflect the other." Cindy believes children are so overscheduled and spend so much time being shuffled from place to place that they often don't know what to do during the rare quiet moment. She stressed that just spending time with your baby, holding her and looking in her eyes, making her feel infinitely loved and cared for will help her immeasurably as she grows older. "There's great value in quiet moments," she noted.

Authors Alvin Rosenfeld and Nicole Wise concur in their book *Hyper-Parenting: Are You Hurting Your Child by Trying Too Hard?* They write, "It is tough to try to be relaxed, especially when we so desperately fear being negligent. What we parents really need as much as, or perhaps even more than, all that important advice about how to raise our children is a reminder that no one ever gets it all just right—and that most children turn out well anyway."

I believe one of the biggest responsibilities parents have is recognizing each child's God-given talents and doing all they can to nurture them. Cindy Giddings agrees. "Find your child's passion and pursue it . . . offer enhancing opportunities when appropriate and easy to do. It doesn't have to be prescheduled," she adds.

"Find your child's passion and pursue it . . . offer enhancing opportunities when appropriate and easy to do."

How does this relate to *Baby Sing & Sign,* you ask? Simply put, you may think the idea of teaching babies to sign is the greatest thing ever. However, be open to the possibility that your infant has other ideas. It may not be her cup of tea. Or it may suit her just fine, but not at eight months, twelve months, or even sixteen. Sign language cannot be force-fed. The beauty of the *Baby Sing & Sign* program is that it can be incorporated into naturally occurring life situations, such as in the car and during mealtimes. Although taking a *Baby Sing & Sign* class is great fun, the program can also be home-based and home-taught.

The information in this book is intended to give you, as teacher-guide, the tools and activities you need to help your baby learn sign language. The rules are not set in stone. The timeline isn't concrete. What worked for your best friend's son may not have any impact on your daughter. That's okay. You have not failed as a parent or teacher and most certainly your child hasn't failed you.

"Expect nothing and you will never be disappointed." How easy that is to say, and how difficult it is to put into daily practice. But for the sake of your children, it's important to try and celebrate the ordinary moments of life with your child without getting too far ahead of yourself in terms of your goals and dreams for baby. Childhood is not merely preparation for the future, but a time that is precious and valuable in its own right.

A SIGN OF SUCCESS

♪ BABIES' SURPRISING RESPONSES ♪

"Ah, music. A magic beyond all we do here!"
—J. K. ROWLING, *HARRY POTTER AND THE SORCERER'S STONE*

There is something mystical and profoundly unpredictable in the ways children begin to express their musical selves. I have never met a baby who doesn't adore music. A child's developing awareness of music in all its forms—from Mozart to Madonna—can provide some remarkable moments for those of us who are fortunate enough to witness them.

Fifteen-month-old Bennett was a confident walker and spent the majority of his time on the move. As a member of a *Baby Sing & Sign* class he was keenly interested in the music and play portion of the program, but seemed only marginally interested in the sign language instruction. His mother, Rebecca, began to teach Bennett some basic sign vocabulary, starting with MORE, MUSIC, and FISH. She was patient and consistent with her signing, but not certain that Bennett was even watching as she signed and spoke. Shortly after starting the class, Rebecca was listening to the funeral ceremony for former President Ronald Reagan on television. Elsewhere in the room, her son was busy playing with his toys as usual and appeared to pay no attention to the television program. But when a choir began to perform during the ceremony, Bennett set down his toys and walked to his mother. He looked at the television set and signed MUSIC. This was an amazing moment for her.

Some scientists suggest that babies are biologically "prewired" to respond to certain classes of sound, and that was perhaps the reason why Bennett recognized that both the choral performance and his baby sign songs were "music." For me, the image of a toddler signing MUSIC for the first time in response to a musical event that occurred in a "picture box," camouflaged in a musical form he had never experienced, is nothing short of miraculous. It reminds me of the difference between thinking and learning. I am humbled with the knowledge that babies are often their own best teachers.

. . . And so grateful to be a part of Bennett's life.

> A child's developing awareness of music in all its forms—from Mozart to Madonna—can provide some remarkable moments for those of us who are fortunate enough to witness them.

BOOKS TO READ

Babies love to look at pictures of other babies. Researchers confirm that babies actually recognize faces better than adults, because their brains enable them to focus on the perceptual differences that are most important for telling human faces apart. As they grow they lose the ability to detect those differences, because they are no longer as useful.

Skidamarink! I Love You by Michael Scott (Hyperion Books for Children) is chock-full of wonderful baby faces and plenty of action for reading and signing, including I LOVE YOU, PLAY, TOY, SLEEP, BOY, and GIRL. The complete performance of this beautiful baby love song is available on various childrens' music recordings. You are your child's musical shining STAR, so snuggle and SING your own special version of this sweet story.

STARS

Five Wishing Stars by Treesha Runnells and Sarah Dillard (Piggy Toes Press)

I Love the Night by Dar Hosta (Brown Dog Books)

Ten Wishing Stars: A Countdown to Bedtime Book by Sarah Dillard (Piggy Toes Press)

Twinkle, Twinkle, Little Star by Iza Trapani and Jane Taylor (Charlesbridge)

The Moon and the Stars by Alona Frankel (HarperFestival)

MOON

Good Night Sun, Hello Moon by Karen Viola (Reader's Digest)

I Love You, Sun, I Love You, Moon by Tomie DiPaola (Putnam Juvenile)

Kitten's First Full Moon by Kevin Henkes (Greenwillow Books)

Over the Moon: An Adoption Tale by Karen Katz (Henry Holt)

Papa Please Get the Moon for Me by Eric Carle (Picture Book Studio)

Rise the Moon by Eileen Spinelli (Dial Books for Young Readers)

The Moon and the Stars by Alona Frankel (HarperFestival)

BLANKET

Baby Duck and the Cozy Blanket by Amy Hest and Jill Barton (Candlewick Press)

Blankie by Leslie Patricelli (Penguin Group)

Blankie: A Book to Touch and Feel by Patricia Ryan Lampl and Valeria Petrone (Little Simon)

Messages from the Heart: My Blanket: Huggable, Lovable, Snuggable Books by Sandra Magsamen (Little, Brown)

Owen by Kevin Henkes (Weston Woods Studio)

I LOVE YOU

I Love You More by Judy Cooley (Shadow Mountain)

I Love You More by Laura Duksta and Karen Keelser (I Shine)

Just in Case You Ever Wonder by Max Lucado (Tommy Nelson)

You Are My I Love You by Mary Ann K. Cusimano and Satomi Ichikawa (Philomel Books)

Give a Little Love by Lizzie Mack (Little Simon)

I Love My Mama by Peter Kavanagh (Simon and Schuster)

I Love Animals by Flora McDonnell (Candlewick Press)

BABY SING & SIGN
DICTIONARY

AIRPLANE

ALL-DONE

APPLE

BALL

BANANA

BED

BLANKET

BOOK

BOY

BUNNY

CAR

CAT

CEREAL

CHAIR

CHEESE

DADDY

DRINK

DOG

EAT

FISH   **FOOD**   **GIRL**

HELP   **HOT**

HURT   **I LOVE YOU**   **MILK**

MOMMY   **MOON**   **MORE**

MUSIC

OUCH

PLAY

PLEASE

SIT

SLEEP

SORRY

STOP

STARS

THANK YOU

TOY

WAGON

WANT

WATER

GLOSSARY

AMERICAN SIGN LANGUAGE (ASL): widely accepted language of deaf culture utilizing gestures.

APPROXIMATION: close resemblance to an object or event (e.g., sign formation, a desired melody).

AUTISM: brain disorder characterized by impairment of social relationships, inappropriate or exaggerated responses to stimuli, and/or abnormal language development.

CAREGIVER: person other than the parent who cares for children (e.g., sitter, other family member).

CAUSE AND EFFECT: understanding that one action results in a reaction or consequence (e.g., if a child pushes a ball, it will roll).

COCHLEAR IMPLANT: hearing aid implanted in the inner ear that restores hearing to some people with hearing loss.

DEVELOPMENTALLY APPROPRIATE: skills or knowledge that fall within the range of what can typically be expected of someone at a certain age.

EXPRESSIVE LANGUAGE: use of words and/or gestures to communicate with others.

MARKED HAND SHAPE: sign language gestures that incorporate a letter of the signed alphabet.

NEOCORTEX: part of the brain that controls thinking (including reasoning, language, and problem solving). It can be physiologically altered through sensory experiences and learning.

NEURAL FIBERS: structures that enable nerve cells (neurons) to transmit signals to and receive signals from other nerve cells. Neural connections are the basis for learning, and experience can change their strength and efficiency.

OBJECT PERMANENCE: a child's ability to understand that objects still exist even when they are no longer in sight. Children younger than eight months typically do not have this ability.

RECEPTIVE LANGUAGE: ability to understand and organize language.

SEQUENCING SKILLS: ability to order objects using a rule or pattern (e.g., smallest to largest).

SYNAPSE: gap between nerve cells (neurons). Neurons communicate with other neurons by electrochemical activity in which various chemicals (neurotransmitters) are fired or sent across synapses. Synaptic activity is a part of learning, indeed of life.

TACTILE STIMULATION: feedback received from touch.

UNMARKED HAND SHAPE: sign language gestures that do not incorporate a letter of the signed alphabet.

Baby Sing & Sign enhances the bond between
parent or caregiver and child.

REFERENCES AND RESOURCES

♪ Sign Language and Child Development

Acredolo, Linda, and Susan Goodwyn. *Baby Minds.* New York: Bantam Books, 2000.
———. *Baby Signs.* Chicago: Contemporary Books, 1996.
Bahan, Ben, and Joe Dannis. *Signs for Me: Basic Sign Vocabulary for Children, Parents, and Teachers.* San Diego, CA: Dawn Sign Press, 1990.
Bailey, Becky. *I Love You Rituals.* New York: Harper Paperbacks, 2000.
Baker, Pamela, and Patricia B. Bellen Gillen. *My First Book of Sign.* Washington, DC: Gallaudet University Press, 2002.
Caton, Carl. "The Four Elements of Effective Family Traditions." *People of Faith.* http://www.peopleoffaith.com/family-traditions.html. Caton Development, 2003.
Chaney, Carolyn. "Young Children's Jokes: A Cognitive Developmental Perspective." Paper presented at the Annual Meeting of the Western States Communication Association (Albuquerque, New Mexico, February 14, 1993).
Cline, Foster, MD, and Jim Fay. *Parenting with Love and Logic.* Colorado Springs, CO: Pinon Press, 1990.
Cohen, Lawrence J. *Playful Parenting: A Bold New Way to Nurture.* New York: Ballantine Books, 2001.
Cohen, Oscar. "The Adverse Implications of Full Inclusion for Deaf Students." Paper presented at the 18th International Congress on Education of the Deaf (Tel Aviv, Israel, July 16–20, 1995).
Cox, Meg. *The Heart of a Family: Searching America for New Traditions That Fulfill Us.* New York: Random House, 1998.
Crain, William. *Reclaiming Childhood.* New York: Henry Holt, 2003.
Daniels, Marilyn. *Dancing with Words: Signing for Hearing Children's Literacy.* Westport, CT: Bergin, and Garvey, 2001.
De Haan, Michelle. "Babies Recognize Faces Better than Adults." *BBC News: Health.* http://news.bbc.co.uk/1/hi/health/1991705.stm. May 16, 2002.

Ezzo, Gary, and Anne Marie. "Preschoolers and the Benefits of Play." *Growing Families International.* http://www.gfi.org/java/jsp/article14.htm.

Gabriel, Jerry. "The Truth about Boys and Girls." *Brain Connection.* www.brainconnection.com/content/91_1. July 2001.

Garcia, Joseph. *Sign with Your Baby: How to Communicate with Infants before They Can Speak.* Seattle, WA: Northlight Communications; Bellingham, WA: Stratton Kehl Publications, 1999.

Garcia, Joseph. "Signing with Children with Special Needs." *Benefits of Signing.* http://www.sign2me.com/benefits.php.

Gardner, Howard. *Frames of Mind.* New York: Basic Books, 1993.

———. *Intelligence Reframed: Multiple Intelligences for the 21st Century.* New York: Basic Books, 2000.

Goodwyn, Susan, and Linda Acredolo, "Encouraging symbolic gestures: effects on the relationship between gesture and speech." In J. Iverson and S. Goldin-Meadows, eds. *The Nature and Functions of Gesture in Children's Communication* (San Francisco: Jossey-Bass, 1998), 61-73.

Golinkoff, Roberta M., and Kathy Hirsh-Pasek. *How Babies Talk: The Magic and Mystery of Language in the First Three Years of Life.* New York: Penguin Group, 1999.

Gopnik, Alison, Andrew N. Meltoff, and Patricia Kuhl. *The Scientist in the Crib: What Early Learning Tells Us about the Mind.* New York: HarperCollins, 1999.

Gurian, Michael. *Boys and Girls Learn Differently!: A Guide for Teachers and Parents.* San Francisco: Jossey-Bass, 2001.

———. *The Wonder of Boys.* New York: Penguin Putnam, 1997.

Hafer, Jan, Robert Wilson, and Paul Setzer. *Come Sign with Us: Sign Language Activities for Children.* Washington, DC: Gallaudet University Press, 2002.

Ledbetter, J. Otis. *Family Traditions: Practical, Intentional Ways to Strengthen Your Family Identity.* Colorado Springs, CO: Cook Communications, 1998.

Miller, Karen. "Caring for the Little Ones: Creative Activities for Infants and Toddlers." *Child Care Information Exchange* 113 (Jan.–Feb. 1997), 35–37.

MacGregor, Cynthia. *Fun Family Traditions.* New York: Meadowbrook Press, 2000.

Michelli, Joseph. *Humor Play and Laughter: Stress-Proofing Life with Your Kids.* Golden, CO: Love and Logic Press, 1998.

Murphy, Lois Barclay, PhD, and Rachel Moon, MD. "Babies and Their Senses." http://www.zerotothree.org/play/. Zero to Three: National Center for Infants, Toddlers, and Families.

Rimm, Sylvia, PhD. *How to Parent So Children Will Learn.* Watertown, WI: Apple, 1990.

Rosenfeld, Alvin, and Nicole Wise. *Hyper-Parenting: Are You Hurting Your Child by Trying Too Hard?* New York: St. Martin's Press, 2000.

Schank, Roger. *Coloring Outside the Lines: Raising a Smarter Kid by Breaking All the Rules.* New York: HarperCollins, 2000.

Slier, Debby. *Animal Signs.* Washington, DC: Gallaudet University Press, 2002.

Standley, Jayne, "The power of contingent music for infant learning." *Bulletin of the Council for Research in Music Education* 147 (Spring 2001), 65–85.

Stewart, David. *American Sign Language the Easy Way.* Hauppauge, NY: Barron's Educational Series, 1998.

Trudo, Richard. "Helping Your Late-Talking Children." Medicinenet.com. http://www.medicinenet.com/script/main/art.asp?articlekey=52130.

♪ Music for Young Children

Appleby, Amy, and Peter Pickow, ed. *The Library of Children's Song Classics.* New York: Amsco, 1993.

Bradford, Louise L., ed. *Sing It Yourself: 220 Pentatonic American Folk Songs.* Sherman Oaks, CA: Alfred Publishing, 1978.

Brown, Marc. *Hand Rhymes.* New York: Penguin Books, 1985.

Campbell, Don. *The Mozart Effect for Children: Awakening Your Child's Mind, Health, and Creativity with Music.* New York: HarperCollins, 2000.

Cole, William, ed. *Folk Songs of England, Ireland, Scotland, and Wales.* Garden City, NY: Doubleday, 1961.

Feierabend, John M., ed. *Music for Very Little People.* New York: Boosey, and Hawkes, 1986.

———. *The Book of Lullabies.* Chicago: GIA Steps, 2000.

———. *The Book of Simple Songs and Circles.* Chicago: GIA Steps, 2000.

———. *The Book of Tapping and Clapping.* Chicago: GIA Steps, 2000.

———. *The Book of Wiggles and Tickles.* Chicago: GIA Steps, 2000.

Fox, Dan, ed. *Go In and Out the Window: An Illustrated Songbook for Young People.* New York: Metropolitan Museum of Art: Henry Holt, 1987.

Glazer, Tom. *Music for Ones and Twos: Songs and Games for the Very Young Child.* New York: Doubleday, 1983.

Langstaff, Nancy, and John Langstaff, eds. *Jim Along, Josie: A Collection of Folk Songs and Singing Games for Young Children.* New York: Harcourt Brace Jovanovich, 1970.

Lomax, John, and Alan Lomax, eds. *Best Loved American Folk Songs.* New York: Grosset and Dunlap, 1947.

———. *Our Singing Country: Folk Songs and Ballads.* New York: Dover, 1941.

Orff-Schulwerk (American Edition). Volume 1. *Music for Children: Preschool.* Ed. Hermann Regner. Miami, FL: Schott Music Corporation, 1982.

Ortiz, John. *Nurturing Your Child with Music: How Sound Awareness Creates Happy, Smart, and Confident Children.* Hillsboro, OR: Beyond Words, 1999.

Piazza, Carolyn L. *Multiple Forms of Literacy: Teaching Literacy and the Arts.* Upper Saddle River, NJ: Prentice-Hall, 1999.

Sandburg, Carl, ed. *The American Songbag.* New York: Harcourt, Brace, and World, 1927.

Seeger, Ruth Crawford, ed. *American Folk Songs for Children.* New York: Doubleday, 1948.

———. *Animal Folk Songs for Children.* Hamden, CT: Linnet Books, 1950.

Simon, William L., ed. *The Reader's Digest Children's Songbook.* Pleasantville, NY: Reader's Digest Association, 1985.

Winn, Marie, ed. *The Fireside Book of Children's Songs.* New York: Simon, and Schuster, 1966.

♪ Web sites

American Sign Language Browser (http://commtechlab.msu.edu/sites/aslweb/browser.htm)
This site provides hundreds of one-word video clips and instruction of ASL signs.

Baby Signs (http://www.babysigns.com/)
The official site for Acredolo and Goodwyn's Baby Signs program.

Baby Sing & Sign (www.babysingandsign.com) and Love Language (www.lovelanguageforbabies.com/)
The official Web site for Baby Sing & Sign *and the Kansas City-based Love Language program. Information about research, classes, and instructional products, as well as articles on getting started signing with babies. Song samples also available here.*

Becky Bailey's Loving Guidance and Conscious Discipline Programs (www.beckybailey.com/)
Information about the programs and products of Becky A. Bailey, PhD, the founder of Loving Guidance, Inc., a company dedicated to creating positive environments for children, families, schools and businesses. Bailey is also the developer of the Conscious Discipline program.

Berkeley Parents Network (http://parents.berkeley.edu/advice/babies/signing.html)
Forum for parents to offer advice and comments about their experiences with baby signing.

Brain Connection (www.brainconnection.com/)
An online source of information about the brain for educators, parents, students, and teachers.

EduScapes: A Site for Life-Long Learners of all Ages (www.eduscapes.com/)
A potpourri of resources and topics for educators.

Handspeak (www.handspeak.com)
Information about baby sign is included at this site for learning visual languages.

John Feierabend's Early Childhood Music Program (www.giamusic.com/)
Information about the philosophy, research, and teaching materials of one of the country's leaders in music for young children.

Kinder Signs: Baby Sign Language University (www.kindersigns.com/)
An Orlando, Florida-based program founded by speech pathologist Diane Ryan devoted to teaching parents how to communicate with their babies before they can speak.

National Institute of Environmental Health Sciences (NIEHS) Kids' Pages (www.niehs.nih.gov/kids)
A wonderful collection of resources for parents and educators, including an index with lyrics for hundreds of childrens' songs. Many include a simple instrumental arrangement to help you learn or recall the melody.

Peggy Seeger (www.pegseeger.com/)

Stories, humor, and information by Ms. Seeger about her experiences as a songwriter, singer, and member of the famous folk-singing Seeger family. Family recordings from the Seeger family (Rounder Records) containing music collected by Ruth Crawford Seeger is also available here, including: American Folk Songs for Children, Animal Folk Songs for Children, *and* American Folk Songs for Christmas.

Real Families (www.real-families.com)

Laura Murphy, program founder, uses real-life examples and expectations to provide parenting, marriage, and family education. Classes and individual coaching are available.

Sign 2 Me (www.sign2me.com/)

Information about Joseph Garcia's "Sign with Your Baby" program.

Signing Baby (http://www.signingbaby.com/main/)

Created by a signing mother, this Web site includes articles, signing stories, and photographs of babies signing.

A child is never too young to develop a love for books and reading.

ABOUT THE AUTHOR

ANNE MEEKER MILLER, PhD, is the founder of the Love Language program. She teaches *Baby Sing & Sign* series and seminars at a major medical center in the Kansas City area. Through her writing and workshops, she shares information about the benefits of music, sign language, and play for babies and gives easy and practical strategies for integrating all three into the daily lives of families.

Anne is a music therapist for the early childhood special education program of the Blue Valley School District in Overland Park, Kansas. Her preschool students were the inspiration for her work with sign language and music. Anne observed the way song and sign positively impacted the language skills of her students and wanted to have an even earlier influence in the lives of children when language is first acquired.

Anne has taught music to students from preschool through college levels. She received the Excellence in Teaching award given by the Learning Exchange, Kansas City Chamber of Commerce, and the *Kansas City Star*. She was a commission member of the Housewright Symposium on the Future of Music Education sponsored by the Music Educators National Conference. Anne lives in Olathe, Kansas, where she enjoys spending time with her husband, three sons, and Wheaten terrier, Cooper.

CONTRIBUTORS

♪ Carrie Kent, Coauthor of "A Sign of Success" Stories

Carrie has extensive experience as a writer, editor, and proofreader for a variety of print publications, including magazines, newspapers, and newsletters. She writes about real estate for the *Kansas City Star*. Her earlier professional experience included stints as an associate editor for the *Mother Earth News* and as a research and administrative assistant for two prominent columnists in the Washington, DC, bureau of the *Wall Street Journal*. She has also been employed as a live-in nanny (among the happiest years of her life) and continues to work as a babysitter with Nannies of Kansas City, Ltd. Carrie's child-care experience and writing skills have come together for this project of describing the wonderful world of babies who learn to sign through music and play.

When she isn't working, writing, or playing with children, Carrie enjoys baking, cooking, and decorating her home. Her four pets keep her busy, as does corresponding with close friends who live in other states.

♪ Jeff Petrie, Illustrator

Jeff Petrie has been interested in drawing ever since he was a child. He studied graphic design at Johnson County Community College in Overland Park, Kansas. A piece of his artwork was featured at the Muscular Dystrophy Association national headquarters, and his Christmas card illustration was chosen for the Muscular Dystrophy Association's Holiday Wishes Collection in 2000 and 2003. Jeff received the MDA Personal Achievement award for the Kansas City area and the state of Kansas in 2001.

Jeff enjoys listening to and collecting music, going to concerts, surfing the Internet, and hanging out with friends. He lives in Overland Park, Kansas, with his family and two dogs, Einstein and Hailey. His whimsical illustrations are a wonderful addition to this book.

Amy Martin, Photographer

After a previous life as a computer software designer and several wonderful years at home raising her three beautiful daughters, Amy Martin decided to follow her passion and began a new career as a portrait photographer. With the encouragement and support of her family and friends, she started a small studio in the Kansas City area, where she spends her time capturing the magic and innocence of small children.

Amy lives in Olathe, Kansas, with her husband, daughters, and a small menagerie of four-legged friends. Her photographs are a wonderful enhancement for this program and get to the heart of the playfulness and fun we aspire to share with our readers.

ACKNOWLEDGMENTS

The following "cast" of performers, editors, and parenting experts deserve a standing ovation for their help with this project: Colette Barnes-Maelzer, Julie Broski, Terry Busch, Dr. David Circle, Dr. Cindy Colwell, Dr. Sue Denny, Judi Farinelli, Marjorie Gamble, Charles Golladay, Loni Herrera, Mary Licktieg, Kirsten McBride, Robin Olson, Gayle Kebodeux, Kim Tappan, Dr. David Wagner, and Wendy Webb. A "group hug" goes out to the parents and children of the Blue Valley School District and my *Baby Sing & Sign* class participants.

Thanks to all of those whose photographs appear in the book: Megan and William Baum; Jack Bryan; Brad, Isaac, and Kendall Burr; Marlin and Tabitha Burt; Ava Clayton; Anthony and Edda Concessi; Josie and Max Faoro; Gilli Gerson; Brady Hale; Ella Hans; Kreg and Lana Herman; Jaylie Hicklin; Edie Howard; Jillian Lewis; Allison and Karen McNellis; Turi and Al Melichar; Heather Metcalf; Greg, Kevin, Andy, and Cooper Miller; Ermil Miller; Anna Munley; Peyton Ott; Jaclynn Pickens; Justa, Keith, Lea, and Richard Plantenberg; Deirdre Poague; Lucy and Tracy Powell; Mac Rodrick; Naomi Routien; Gianni and Isabella Scavuzzo; Nathan and Nicholas Siscoe; Andrew Stark; Hannah and Melinda Young; as well as Megan Hankins and Lana Herman, my sign language "super models."

Love and gratitude to Cindy Giddings for building *Baby Sing & Sign* with me, and to "Team *BS&S*" for expert counsel, hand-holding, hard work, and dreaming out loud with me: Darcy Beaver, Kendall Burr, Jennifer Ferguson, Barb Harper, Amy Scavuzzo, and Melinda Young.

I thank Pola Firestone for teaching the teacher to be an author, and Carrie Kent for loving this project as much as its "mother" does. Thanks to all of my musical men for their incredible talent, creativity, and good humor: Rick Burch, Richard McCroskey, Mike Nicholis, and my muse, Kelly Werts. "Bravo" to Dr. Rudolf E. Radocy for his assistance with the glossary and his wise reminder that "complex things can only be simplified so far." I am grateful to Alice-Ann Darrow, my official cheerleader as well as my wonderful "other mother," Loretta Miller, and her sweet husband, Ermil. Love and gratitude to my sister, Donna, who is the woman I want to be when I grow up.

This book would still be just a twinkle in my eye if my literary agent, Neil Salkind, hadn't gently nudged me into the marketplace. I want to express my gratitude to him for believing in this book without hesitation, and for his uncanny ability to read my mind. Thanks also to my editor, Katie McHugh, for asking all the questions I forgot to answer and for being perfectly suited to guide this project.

Most of all, I thank my prince-of-a-husband, Dan, and our fine "babies" Greg, Kevin, and Andy, who have been an unwavering cheering section for all things *Baby Sing & Sign*. "I love you more than a thousand Table Rock Lakes."

Coming Summer 2007

TODDLER SING & SIGN®

Animals & Colors
Learning Signs the Fun Way through Music and Play

ANNE MEEKER MILLER, PhD

FEATURING:

○ 2006 Parents' Choice and 2006 National Parenting
  Publications award-winning "Bright-Eyed and Bushy-
  Tailed" music CD
○ More than 50 words and signs to learn
○ Instructional black & white photos throughout
○ Signing games, play activities, and more

208 pages | $17.95 | Paperback and Audio CD | 978-1-60094-020-0

Marlowe & Company
Available wherever books are sold
www.marlowepub.com
www.babysingandsign.com